TO LIVE HEROICALLY

SUNY Series,
The Social Context of Education

Christine E. Sleeter, Editor

TO LIVE HEROICALLY

Institutional Racism and American Indian Education

Delores J. Huff

STATE UNIVERSITY OF NEW YORK PRESS

Production by Ruth Fisher
Marketing by Bernadette LaManna

Published by
State University of New York Press, Albany

For information, address the State University of New York Press,
State University Plaza, Albany, NY 12246

Library of Congress Cataloging-in-Publication Data

Huff, Delores J.
    To live heroically : institutional racism and American Indian
education / Delores J. Huff.
        p.   cm. — (SUNY series, the social context of education)
    Includes index.
    ISBN 0-7914-3237-8 (hardcover : alk. paper), — ISBN 0-7914-3238-6
(pbk. : alk. paper)
    1. Indians of North America—Education.   2. Indians of North
America—Government policy.   3. Indians of North America—Social
conditions.   4. Education and state—United States—History.
5. Discrimination in education—United States—History.   6. United
States. Bureau of Indian Affairs—History.   7. United States—
Social policy.   8. United States—Race relations.   I. Title.
    II. Series: Suny series, social context of education.
E97.H78   1997
370'.8997—dc20   96-12965
                                                                            CIP

10 9 8 7 6 5 4 3 2 1

Self Concept

For many children
the school is the focal point
for the development of functional self-esteem.
By functional we mean
the feeling of empowerment that allows one to:
Take the responsibility for one's life
To live by one's own standard
To be honest about one's feelings
To give love
To receive love
To live productively—give all you've got—give 100 percent
To take risks
To make commitments
TO LIVE HEROICALLY

Anne Ninham Medicine, Seneca
Stanford University

DEDICATION

To the generations of Indian children—who endured history classes extolling the heroism of Christopher Columbus (who enslaved and slaughtered the Arawak to extinction)—who have learned from history books that label Indians as savages and pagans (and perpetuate a modern cultural genocide to rationalize the historical physical genocide)—who endured the ignominy of having to wear turkey feathered headdresses in class in celebration of Thanksgiving Day (and the historical amnesia of the genocide perpetrated by the puritans and pilgrims on the Wampannoags, the Massachusetts, the Narragansetts, the Schaghticokes, and many of the eastern tribes that lived in New England thousands of years before the Puritans landed on Plymouth Rock)—who in their confusion and bewilderment watch western movies and root for the cowboys.

In spite of it all, each generation of Indians has survived and endured the pain. We adult Indians know how painful it is to be a nonperson in our own country. All pain comes to an end. Sooner or later, you either die from pain or develop antibodies to withstand the virus of cultural invasion. My generation wants the pain to end, so that your generration can bring sanity into the twenty first century.

If life is really a crap shoot, my bet is on you.

CONTENTS

ACKNOWLEDGMENTS

Somewhere in the recesses of my memory zone (or what Hercule Poirot calls "the little gray cells" I recall a rumor that Hemingway wrote his books standing up, pen in hand and never re-wrote. I have a suspicion that either he started that rumor himself, or had a damn good editor. No writer stands alone . . . without the heroic efforts of editors.

I was fortunate in that my first editor, Tom Moradian knew where I wanted to go with my words, and gingerly guided me along. I owe him a great debt of gratitude for his professionalism and TLC. An eagle feather to you, Tom.

Christine Sleeter was absolutely wonderful in the insights she gave me as she brought this book to its final stage. Her skill as an editor and an academician was essential to making this book readable to the lay person, and significant to the academicians. There is an eagle feather that is given to an honored woman, a woman of substance. It is the only feather that is perfectly straight. I wish this to you, Christine, a woman of substance. Thank you.

INTRODUCTION

The origins of universal American public education began with a somewhat vague concept of 'meritocracy', an institution with the potential of weaving a cultural tapestry out of the raw illiterates of the world and forging a nation of educated middle-class Americans. This contemporary social institution often ignited communities precisely because of the unspoken promise it made to families that each succeeding generation would have economic and social advantages heretofore denied because of rigid class structure buttressed by an exclusionary education system. Every family had ambitions for their children, and for many, the institution of education held to their promise. But there is a growing number of children born with innate gifts who will never realize their potential.

In spite of parental ambitions, children perceive and internalize impressions of their future in the classroom. With each succeeding year in school, these perceptions, like the shell of a turtle, solidify. By the time a youngster reaches puberty, the shell has hardened and shaped his or her tacit understanding of the world, the future, and expected role he or she will play as an adult. Without a doubt, parents can play a significant role in the development of self-esteem in children, but sadly these efforts can be seriously undermined in the classroom.

Ideally, education reinforces parental infusion of self-worth and competence, as children progress from the raw material of a kindergartner into the finished product of a competent twelfth grader. That is the ideal. However, some children, are left out of the ideal. For those young people, education inculcates despair and a bleak perception of their future.

There has been little change in the data since the last significant national survey conducted by Alexander Astin on high-school drop-out rates. That study reported the mean drop-out rate for whites as 17.8 percent, African Americans 39.4 percent, Chicanos 49.7 percent, Puerto Ricans at 52.5 percent and (estimated) American Indians at 50 percent.[1] Even these figures mask the whole story, because minorities who graduate do not receive the same quality education as their white colleagues.

Education is a political act. Access or lack of access to quality education is a political decision. We spend more money on bombs than on classrooms because the defense lobby in Washington, D.C., has more political clout than the education lobby. Every educational appropriation by Congress, by the state legislation, by the county and city you live in is determined by political leverage, not by the goal of developing a society of critical thinkers. As a nation, we are very suspect of intellectuals and reward them only marginally. Teachers are paid less than garbage workers. We are a "nation at risk," as reported by Terrel Bell, because we have settled for mediocrity in our education system. To paraphrase Bell, minorities are especially at risk, because institutional racism is endemic in school systems.[2] Even today there are minorities who have never seen a teacher, principal, or superintendent of their race in any school they have attended. While we have made inroads to generate role models for our children, those hired are too few to provide role models for minority children.

The politics of American education replicates the caste and class system of American society. Minority children continue to have the highest dropout rates and the lowest scholastic achievement scores. They, as their parents, are destined to live their lives at or below the poverty levels and suffer from a high rate of unemployment.

Many states have an equalization policy that subsidizes educational resources for poorer communities, but in practical application, poor communities receive fewer resources and, in fact, expect less achievement from minority students, than those in richer (predominantly white) communities. Poor ethnic communities still receive less care, concern, and commitment for education than middle-class white communities. In the Reagan era, we heard the secretary of education argue that we are throwing away millions on education; in the same cabinet, the secretary of defense justified spending six hundred dollars per toilet seat for the Air Force.

The politics of education can be so subtle that we do not realize how this institution carefully indoctrinates the young to the values of previous generations. Nor do we separate the mythology from the reality of education. Mythology says that it is a leveling field, where class or status is secondary to meritocracy. The reality is that schools predict whether a student will be a factory worker or a doctor, and invariably the income of the parents is the correlating factor. The now-classic studies of Michael Katz and Robert Rosenthal of two communities—one poor one wealthy—near Boston have been replicated by others. Michael Katz hypothesized that the faculty and curriculum of a school system in a poor white community of Boston rewarded hard work, attention to instruction, conformity, rote learning, and punctuality which, he said, are exactly the characteristics local factories rewarded in their work force.[3] Rosenthal targeted a wealthy community in the surrounding Boston area and found that teachers and curricula were organized around the likelihood that more than 90 percent of the student body would go to college. In this system, rewards went to students who were original thinkers, creative, analytical, and eclectic.[4] The evidence marshaled by both of these studies says that education systems predict the economic and social adult roles of students by selecting and sanctioning behaviors corresponding to class and caste.

The politics of education to indoctrinate class and caste is even more transparent in Indian Country.[5] It was not the individual states, but the federal government itself who subsidized mission schools, the objective of which was not education, but indoctrination concerning colonization into generations of young Indians. The U.S. Constitution distancing church from state was conveniently set aside during the Indian mission-school era. These schools were supported by federal funds, and later these subsidies went to build and operate federal manual-labor Indian day schools and off-reservation boarding schools.

As this book will show, those in charge of educating Indians began with the premise that Indians were intellectually inferior to whites and incapable of critical thinking. It will demonstrate the racial chauvinism used to justify the deprivation of Indian political rights, the confiscation of tribal personal property, and, when education failed to instill subservience, genocide.

While others might have expressed the same thoughts privately,[6] Andrew Jackson publicly demanded the removal of Indians as impediments to nationhood. Couched as "western movement" this rationale is found in American history textbooks widely used in school today. Jackson advanced the argument of Vattel, a Swiss Philosopher, the land should go to the ones who make it the most productive. Vattel also believed that Indians were savages and did not appreciate the wealth of their homelands.[7]

In 1830, Jackson went before Congress to make his plea for

Indian removal: "What good man, demanded Andrew Jackson, would prefer a country covered with forests and ranged by a few thousand savages to our extensive Republic, studded with cities and towns, and prosperous farms, embellished with all the improvements which art can devise or industry execute, occupied by more than 12,000,000 happy people, and filled with all the blessings of liberty, civilization, and religion?[8]

Chief Justice Marshall of the U.S. Supreme Court, declared Indian removal unconstitutional. Jackson is said to have remarked "Well, let him enforce it."[9]

Who were these "savages" Jackson targeted for removal from the eastern corridor? They were powerful and prosperous Indian nations, too powerful and far too prosperous for the American citizen. One of the largest, the Cherokee, were wealthy farmers. The Cherokee Nation engaged in extensive international trade, owned businesses, provided tribal social services, and operated two hundred bilingual schools.[10] Cherokee independence was legendary. They had long since left behind the simple wigwam of the eighteenth century and built homes much like those of their white neighbors.

Who were the 12 million "happy people" that Jackson extolled? He led Congress to believe they were small farmers and ranchers. In reality, they were industrialists and entrepreneurs who coveted Indian lands for their gold, coal, iron ore, and timber. In fact, the forces that led to removal did not come, as historian Van Every wrote,

> from the poor white frontiersmen who were neighbors of the Indians. They came from the industrialization and commerce, the growth of populations, of railroads and cities, the rise in value of land, and the greed of businessmen. Party managers and land speculators manipulated the growing excitement, . . . press and pulpit whipped up the frenzy. Out of that frenzy, the Indians were to end up dead or exiled, the land speculators richer, the politicians more powerful. As for the poor white frontiersmen, he played the part of a pawn, pushed into the first violent encounters, but soon dispensable.[11]

Another example of Jackson's hypocrisy was his denunciation of the Iroquois as "savage." They fought for their homelands with all of their might, which was the real reason Jackson wanted them removed from the East. But the pejorative term *savage* can hardly be used against a confederation that demonstrated the feasibility of balancing a strong central government with equally sovereign states, a model of constitutional government adopted by the new United States.

There were a few who were opposed to Jackson's Removal Act in Congress. Notably, Senator Frelinghuysen (1830), who said:

> However mere human policy, or the law of power, or the tyrant's pleas of expediency, may have found it convenient at any or in all times to recede from the unchangeable principles of external justice, no argument can shake the political maxim, that, where the Indian always has been, he enjoys an absolute right still to be, in the free exercise of his own modes of thought, government and conduct.[12]

Opposed to removal as he was, Frelinghuysen was nonetheless a staunch supporter of Indian education as a means "to teach them agriculture and the domestic arts; to encourage them to that industry which alone can enable them to maintain their place in existence; and to prepare them in time for that society, which, to bodily comforts, adds the improvement of the mind and morals."[13]

Agriculture certainly did not need to be taught to the Indians, for it was Indians' crops Americans consumed daily. Federal education systems were set up as "pacification" manual-labor training schools as an alternative to underwriting the expense of a standing army and/or annihilation of the Indian. Annual reports from the Indian service to Congress measured success in educating the Indians by the number of Indians working for white farmers, as household help in white homes, and as workers in white-factories.

The necessity for Indian nations to develop a work force in concert with tribal economic development was dismissed as irrelevant (and probably dangerous) by federal policy makers. Today, after a two-hundred-year legacy of federally controlled subsidized education, Indians have a minuscule professional class who are responsible for a mineral resource contract, can build a bridge, can deliver babies, or can run a cottage industry. The politically motivated system did its job well—most Indians have the skills sufficient for manual labor, and only manual labor.

Indian Country needs well-trained professionals who can bring reservations from the preindustrial age into the posttechnological age. Instead, most reservations today rely upon well-trained white professionals to meet the most elementary needs: teachers, administrators, health providers.

Skeptics argue that the past is behind us, but the legacy of economic exploitation by corporate America continues.[14] Replacing yesterday's blatant Jacksonian confiscation of tribal lands are today's energy corporations. These nefarious robber barons are in league with the Bureau of Indian Affairs (BIA), an agency that is supposed to defend Indian rights but that persuades tribes to sign contracts exploiting tribal raw materials in return for a fraction of their real value. And to make it ever easier for these corporations, the federal government subsidizes both the labor costs and the capital equipment for companies doing business on Indian reservations.

The argument is that these energy-based economic activities will improve the living conditions of Indians on the reservations. Under the watchful eye of the Bureau of Indian Affairs, the Senate was astonished to uncover evidence that some of the world's largest energy corporations were systematically cheating tribes out of royalties. During the May 1989 hearings, Kenneth M. Ballen, chief counsel of the Investigations Subcommittee of the Senate Select Committee on Indian Affairs reported: "In a number of instances, the oil company employees were found to be under reporting the amount of oil and gas being taken from the Indian lands what one investigator described as a very sophisticated kind of theft. They may slightly mis-measure the amount of oil they take out. Maybe they mis-measure it by a barrel, one of 100 barrels—but if you do that every single time—it adds up."[15]

Indian Country may be rich in minerals, but the profitable bonanza goes to these corporations, not to the tribes. That may be a minor complaint compared to the ecological and environmental damage these corporations leave behind. The Navajo Nation has sued Kerr McGee for thirty-five wrongful deaths because this corporation left on their reservation open-pit uranium mines and huge deposits of tailings.[16]

Other tribes have sued the Bureau of Indian Affairs for the mismanagement of their timber resources. The Menominee and Siletz for example, have won law suits against the bureau because of negligence in carrying out their fiduciary responsibilities.[17]

In 1977, the American Indian Policy Review Commission reported: "Indian forestry lands are the largest private holdings of forested and commercial forest land in the United States. One fourth of all Indian lands are forested, and 10 percent of all Indian lands are commercial forest lands. Timber contributes from 25 to 100 percent of tribal revenues, for 5 reservations; more than 80 percent on 11 of these reservations. Income from stumpage (standing trees) alone for 1974 was 73 million."

Nevertheless, at present the potential yield of Indian timber lands is now being achieved. However, it is estimated that the 5

million derived from stumpage sales was 20 percent less than could
have been obtained. This problem is compounded by the fact that
the BIA has failed to implement reforestation and precommercial
thinning programs for many tribal forests.[18]

Some Indians were optimistic after the 1978 American Indian
Policy Review Commission published its findings. Here, in print,
was documented evidence of Indian complaints, gathered by congressional as well as Indian staff. An example reported by the commission was the BIA's management of the Quinault reservation
in Washington:

> The annual allowable cut on the Quinault Reservation is 200
> million board-feet. Actual harvest in 1975 was only 122 million
> board-feet. The Quinault estimate is that a properly managed
> forestry program would yield for stumpage alone an income
> of $22 million in 1976 prices for the Quinault Tribe. Develop-
> ment of tribal forestry management capabilities, logging oper-
> ations, sawmills and manufacturing plants using sawmill
> products would generate 1,800 jobs in the timber industry
> alone. It is estimated for every job in the timber industry, 1.8
> jobs are established in related industries. Maximization of the
> Quinault timber industry would thus translate to some 5,360
> jobs throughout the Quinault region, . . . generating an excess
> of 70 million in the region.[19]

The Quinault resent the BIA leases because they do not benefit
from them either with a reasonable level of income or with jobs.
Congress was also unhappy with the cost of providing basic support
for unemployed Indians. Logically, these two factors should have
combined to effect a change in tribal leasing contracts. Not so. Five
years later, Joe De La Cruz, tribal chairman of the Quinault, testified
before the Senate Committee on Indian Affairs, oversight hearings:

> Despite the tremendous contributions of Indian timber to the
> State economy, our people were receiving only a small share
> of the benefits. Non-Indian firms harvested and processed
> nearly all of our timber. Unemployment rates for Indian people
> on those five reservations (Colville, Yakima, Quinault, Makah
> and Spokane) averaged more than 30 percent for the entire
> county, there were only 2,500 man hours of employment in
> forestry, logging and manufacturing while more than 5,000
> jobs in those industries were being supported by the five
> reservations in the State of Washington alone. There were

21,490,000 acres of forests needing thinning on those five reservations, yet only 3,600 acres were thinned. There were 23,000 acres needing reforestation, yet only 152 were planned. . . . In 1981, there was a reported vacancy rate of 16% in Indian forestry positions and about 50% of the vacancies were at the professional level. Only 34 of 337 professional forestry positions in the BIA are currently filled by Indians.[20]

It is unconscionable federal policy to permit this colonial ethic to continue. This tribe needs only a tribal education system to support training in the harvesting, manufacturing, and retailing of its timber and capital to buy the equipment and training necessary. Because this tribe lacks capital for machinery and to hire their own timber professionals they are unable to exercise their legal right under the Self-determination Act to operate a tribal timber industry. Instead they must rely upon the Bureau of Indian Affairs to lease timber rights to major multinational timber corporations, for which the tribe receives a fraction of the income and jobs available.

Reservations play a large role in supplying the nation's energy needs. The Navajo use their scarce water resources for gasification plants at Four Corners to fill the energy needs of Los Angeles, Las Vegas, and Phoenix, yet half of the Navajo homes are without electricity or running water:

Gulf Oil uranium mine shafts "de-watered" wells designed to pump five thousand gallons per minute from the sinking water table in order to expedite the removal of an estimated fifty thousand tons of uranium ore. On paper, at least, the Navajo should be one of the wealthiest people on the earth; in fact (according to the U.S. Civil Rights Commission), they are the poorest ethnic group in the United States, with the great majority living well below poverty level. About one house in five has electricity, and the average per capita income remains more or less steady at nine hundred dollars a year, largely because of the ludicrous terms in the leases signed by the Tribal Council, with the encouragement and approval of the BIA; here again one must conclude that the BIA and the Department of the Interior have made rich white men that much richer at the expense of the helpless and destitute people they were sworn to protect. (In 1975, for example, the Navajo were paid sixty cents a pound for uranium ore that sold for twice that much on the open market, in 1977, Utah International, on the basis of a contract signed twenty years before, was paying royalties of fifteen to thirty-seven cents a ton for strip-mined coal worth fifteen to twenty dollars."[21]

Matthiessen labels these contracts signed by the tribal council as "ludicrous," but this is the legacy of educational colonialism. Generations of Indians have been educated into a subservient mentality, believing in white technological superiority rather than themselves. Some Indians, of course, reject subservience, but many are indoctrinated into believing they cannot operate their own energy resources, timber industries, and commercial fishing enterprises. At this juncture, they may be right. We do not have educated Indians sufficiently trained in these economic activities, and the future does not look promising without radical changes in federal Indian education policies.

A White House Conference on Indian Education was held in January 1992. The final chapter of this book will discuss some of the issues presented, all of which had to do with exerting considerable Indian control over Indian education. Perhaps the Indian-led resolutions will result in legislation nurturing tribal development. Perhaps we will once again see blame placed on the victim by public and state school administrators and Bureau of Indian Affairs and Department of Education officials. Historically, those responsible are the least likely to accept responsibility and/or propose changes.

One policy change that would immediately increase Indian self-esteem would be to force corporate textbook publishers to publish an honest survey of American history. The westward movement, the Indian Wars, the gold rush, and the justification of all these historical movements as necessary for nationhood are gross and racist distortions of history. For example, Indian children in the Ferndale school system of Washington State (three miles from the Lummi Indian reservation) were given social-studies sheets entitled "Mountain Men and Their Women." Underneath the title was the caption (William Lacey, the author of *Skins,* used his own research while writing this essay).

The trappers of the Far West, as rugged and primitive as they were, could not resist the security and affection of a good woman. Finding white women too frail and in short supply, they courted, loved and often married native women they encountered in the West. While trapping in the Rockies they met Indian squaws. While in the Southwest villages, and on Southern California ranches they found attractive Mexican women.

The trappers usually met the squaws at the annual early summer rendezvous. After completing the trading during the first
few days, trappers loosened up for a rip-roaring time sustained
by gallons of lethal alcohol and sadistic games. The Indian
squaw provided "solace of the flesh" when needed. Her availability and different moral code (prostitution was void of moral
taint) were reasons for her popularity. If the relationship grew
into a love-match, the trapper began looking for other qualities. Hopefully, she could cook, sew and work for him to make
his life more comfortable. Domestic chores never really
appealed to any mountain man, and, besides, the squaw was
hardened to harsh labor because of her usual low status in
the tribe.[22]

A student came to my university office recently to complain
that her teacher-education preschool class proposed using the ditty
"Ten little Indians, all in a row, one was shot down, nine more to
go" as a means of teaching subtraction to preschoolers. Several
years ago there was a computer arcade game on the market, the
object of which is how often George Armstrong Custer trapped and
raped Indian women.[23]

There are countless, mindless examples of how distorted history texts have found their way into the American mainstream.
Americans have grown up believing Western movies are factual
and that textbooks are historical truths. Social studies excludes the
history of a race existing an estimated forty-thousand years on this
continent. Excluded also are the accomplishments of Indians that
built cities, codified laws, produced 48 percent of the world's crops,
built seaworthy boats, mapped out roads and trade routes, practiced
medicine, and invented tools still used today.

Generations of Indian children have gone through school confused and fragmented. The commercial images that surround young
Indians are logos for products that represent purity and integrity
(Land O' Lakes products, Mutual of Omaha) and strength (Cleve-
land Indians, and so on). Before the "enlightenment" (pre-1980s)
they read textbooks that referred to them as savages, beasts to be
exterminated, pagans, and uncivilized. Currently, Indians are
depicted as historic artifacts, or are represented in children's stories
as if the modern Indian does not exist. The hidden and mixed
messages Indian children receive tear away at the fiber of their
self-esteem.

Indian parents believe that their children's lives will be different than theirs. They have faith that the education system will

provide a foundation for their children to take control over their lives, to assume responsible and challenging futures. But these illusions are soon shattered when children report racist events that occur regularly and they know that the same experiences they had growing up are hurting their children today. Worse yet, the system is priming their children for the role of servants, for jobs rather than careers. Schools blame Indian parents for failures. They assert parents do not care about education. Nothing could be further from the truth.

In the sixties, the Indian mobilized and targeted the politics of education as the battleground for change. Senator Robert Kennedy, chairman of the Senate Select Committee on Indian Affairs, visited the Bureau of Indian Affairs boarding schools at the invitation of the Indians. His reaction sent tidal waves through the halls of the bureau, and before long he convened congressional hearings on Indian education. His death almost dashed the hopes of Indian Country, but his brother Senator Edward Kennedy took up the gauntlet. Four years later, Congress passed the Indian Education Act in 1972. Hopes were high, and Indian Country pushed further for the passage of the Indian Self-Determination and Education Assistance Act of 1975. Under provisions of both acts, tribal governments had the legal authority to direct and control education as well as any other tribal program formerly administered by the bureau.

In the eighties, the pendulum swung the other way. Congress now had the ear of social scientists hired by federal and state agencies. They claimed that Indians were not ready and were not administratively trained to run tribal schools. Health agencies reported that Indian alcoholism was widespread and the Indian population too unstable to manage sophisticated health and education programs. And finally, accountants from federal and state agencies reported that Indians did not handle budgets very well. The three-pronged attack on Indian self-determination found fertile soil during the Reagan administration.

The cork was out of the bottle, and Indian activism was on the rise. In the eighties it was not politically safe to use the same tactics as those used by former administrations to gain or maintain control over Indian lands and resources. The Reagan administration, wary of mounting a frontal attack but determined to access Indian resources, chose an indirect attack to subdue, or at least neutralize, tribal sovereignty. They used the old tried and true strategy of assembling task forces and research reports to justify wresting control from tribal governments. They focused on two areas: tribal economic development and Indian-controlled schools.

There were numerous studies and reports on development and education during this period, but the most widely disseminated was the American Indian Economic Development Commission report on the use of Indian resources and the ABT Associates report on Indian-controlled schools. To avoid the claim of racial bias, both studies were conducted with Indian participation. Ross Swimmer, former principal chief of the Cherokee Nation was appointed by the White House to head up the American Indian Economic Development Commission.[24] Congress asked the Department of Education to study the cost effectiveness of tribal schools. When the Department of Education officials secured the services of ABT Associates of Cambridge, Massachusetts, they insisted upon full participation of the tribal schools studied. These are only two of the many task forces or studies conducted with the real purpose of justifying eliminating/reducing Indian self-determination.

Indian Country learned some valuable lessons from the past. Every time tribal governments exercised their legal right to autonomy and community control, influence peddlers lobbied Congress to reverse the trend.

It was only one hundred years ago that Senator Dawes of Massachusetts paid a visit to the Cherokee reservation, which at that time was Indian Territory. The pressures for statehood (Oklahoma), the oil interests, and homesteaders persuaded Dawes to frame and lobby for the Dawes Allotment Act. Tribal lands were to be divided up, tribal government disbanded, and the BIA administer tribal programs. The justification for this land grab was that private property would change Indians into capitalists, making it easier to assimilate into mainstream society. The outcome of this contorted social management theory was that Indians lost 86 million acres, or 60 percent of their tribal lands.

Dawes's argument before Congress was interesting. He recounted his visit to the Cherokee reservation and said he observed with his own eyes that the Cherokee Nation was too self-sufficient. It ran its own schools and economic infrastructure and provided housing and food for its members. Cherokees "want for nothing" said Dawes. Dawes felt the prerequisite of civilization was capitalism and the prerequisite of capitalism was individualism. Assimilation would never come about unless individual Indians owned private property. In his words:

> To bring him out of savagery into citizenship we must make the Indian more intelligently selfish before we can make him unselfishly intelligent. We need to awaken in him wants. In

his dull savagery he must be touched by the wings of the divine angel of discontent. Then he begins to look forward, to reach out. The desire for property of his own may become an intense educating force. The wish for a home of his own awakens him to new effort. Discontent with the teepee and the starving rations of the Indian camp in winter is needed to get the Indian out of the blanket and into trousers—and trousers with a pocket in them, and with a pocket that aches to be filled with dollars.[25]

Senator Teller of Utah opposed Dawes on the floor of the Senate. He said Dawes knew nothing about Indians and denounced this social-management theory as one coming from a "lobby of speculative philanthropists." Most basic of all, Teller charged, the main purpose of the bill was not to help the Indians, but to open the reservations to white settlement:

If this were done in the name of Greed, it would be bad enough, but to do it in the name of Humanity and under the cloak of ardent desire to promote the Indian's welfare by making him like ourselves, whether he will or not, is infinitely worse. Of all the attempts to encroach upon the Indian, this attempt to manufacture him into a white man by an Act of Congress and the grace of the Secretary of Interior is the baldest, boldest, and the most unjustifiable.[26]

The pattern is clear. Tribal sovereignty is very threatening to policy makers. The moment tribes provide concrete evidence that they can manage their own reservations, Congress passes legislation such as that of Dawes and in 1953 the Termination Act, which was an attempt to break up reservation lands again into individual allotments. Indians resisted the implementation of the Termination Act. The activism of the fifties and sixties has not dissipated. Why then did the tribal schools agree to participate in the ABT study, especially when the focus was primarily on "cost effectiveness"? It is likely these schools saw their future funding tied to cooperating with the congressional mandate, and equally as likely they saw the possibility of exercising some influence on the scope and content of the study.

Around the same time another study was being conducted, the Madison study, the focus of which was the quality of education Indian children were receiving in a rural public school largely funded through Indian education funds. An analysis of these studies will come in later chapters. Both studies had two factors in common:

the source of educational funds came from Indian education entitlements, and the student population was primarily Indian. From there, the studies deviate remarkably.

The ABT study was conducted by experienced, well-trained, non-Indian researchers, while the Madison study was conducted by myself and two other well-trained experienced Indian woman educators. The student population in the ABT study was completely Indian, while the Madison student population was 70 percent Indian. The ABT study focus compared tribal schools with public and BIA schools in terms of cost effectiveness. The Madison study compared the performance of Indians in public school with students in public schools throughout the state in terms of the quality of education.

The tribal schools participating in the ABT study sought historical data comparing Indian student achievement in the BIA and public schools in their area as part of the study. ABT felt it was outside of the mandate handed down from the Department of Education. This certainly suggests a colonial model of research where the subjects have little or no say in what is being measured or how it is being measured. The Madison study was a collaborative effort between the Indian reservation three miles from the public school, the school board, and the Madison community at large.

ABT used approximately three weeks to conduct their study, the Madison study took eight months. ABT data was generated from existing data, while the Madison data came from extensive interviews of students, parents, teachers, administrators, and community members. The ABT study did not examine the classroom, teacher effectiveness, textbooks, or library. The Madison study did. The Madison study challenges the findings of ABT that Indian students perform better academically in public schools than in Indian controlled schools.

Because of the sensitive nature of the material in the Madison study, the name of the school and the locale will not be revealed; in fact, every effort has been made to conceal the identity of the school. There is no justification for opening up tensions again in this community. I take full responsibility for the evaluations of the academic portion, which includes classroom visitations. The community survey was conducted by my colleagues, but the interpretations and conclusions are mine. In the interest of privacy, although I gratefully acknowledge the help and professionalism of my colleagues, their names will not be revealed.

1

A History of Indians in the Public School System

In its ideal form, the institution of education is a potent liberating force, the highway to autonomy, a means by which individuals actualize and shape a productive and financially secure future. Another, Machiavellian model not easily discerned is one in which legitimate educational goals are submerged to accommodate political ends. In this model, the classroom becomes a battle ground not to actualize but to minimize potential, to inculcate and preserve subservience or a contemporary style of colonialism.

Historically, it is the Machiavellian model most Indians have encountered. Indians were defeated not by military force (although this is widely believed) but by politically restructuring the institution of education to mold a colonial ethos. Colonialism that imprisons young minds with the concept of 'racial/ethnic inferiority' is by far more tyrannical than brute force. Labeled as "pacification," the education developed by missions and the Indian service encouraged young Indian people to lose confidence in their own leaders and their own people and view their history and culture as second-rate. Ultimately, this form of colonialism chipped away at Indian culture, making it more and more difficult for each succeeding generation to lead autonomous and pro-active lives.

The early settlers were the first to encourage Indians to enter their schools. Their motives were not altruistic. Colonists perceived education as a means of separating individual Indians from tribal life and ultimately from tribal lands which the colonists coveted. A few examples of early colonial efforts follow.

1

In 1617 Moore's Charity School (renamed "Dartmouth") was opened in New Hampshire to educate the children of missionaries and American Indians. In 1723, William and Mary College set aside a separate house for Indian students enrolled in the college. John Harvard established scholarship funds for the education of Indian youth. These attempts were not universally accepted by the Indians themselves because even at this early juncture of Indian-white relations, the tribes perceived education as a back door to colonialism. In his essay "Two Tracts," Benjamin Franklin recorded the reaction of some chiefs in Virginia to the offer of educating six Indian youngsters at a college in Williamsburg, Virginia, in 1744:

> . . . Several of our young people were formerly brought up at the colleges of the Northern Provinces. They were instructed in all of your sciences, but when they came back to us they were bad runners; ignorant of every means of living in the woods; unable to bare either cold or hunger; know neither how to build a cabin, take a deer, or kill an enemy; spoke our language imperfectly; were therefore neither fit for hunters, warriors, or counselors; they were totally good for nothing. We are however, not the less obligated by your kind offer, though we must decline it; and to show our grateful sense of it, if the gentlemen of Virginia will send us a dozen of their sons, we will take care of their education, instruct them in all we know and make men of them.[1]

The chiefs' rejection of Virginia's offer came from experience that Indian graduates were poorly trained to contribute to tribal development. This tug of war is the one consistent link throughout the history of Indian education policy. The prevailing wisdom of George Washington and Thomas Jefferson was that by funding missions to educate Indians, tribalism would be eradicated within a few generations. As long as tribalism existed, the Indians would fight to maintain their traditional lands, to which even the earliest settlers admitted they had a legal claim. America was going to wipe out the Indian in the Indian but do it legally, through the education system.

Within a decade after George Washington signed treaties with the Iroquois to fund federal (albeit mission) schools on the reservation, the Eastern tribes began to develop their own education system. The tribally controlled education movement begun in 1802 steadily grew, particularly among the Cherokee and the Choctaw who built and operated tribal schools managed by Indian graduates of Eastern colleges. The Cherokee took umbrage with the curriculum offered Indian students compared to that offered white students. For instance, in 1828 the Cherokee Council wrote a letter to the Mission Board in Boston who were in charge of the Brainerd school on the Cherokee reservation. They warned the board that unless the faculty at Brainerd taught more rigorous academics and less Christian bible, they would close the school down. This was not an idle threat. There were many Cherokee who could teach in a tribal school, and Sequoyah had developed a written Cherokee syllabary in 1820.

A written Cherokee language opened the possibility of developing bilingual textbooks, especially since they now had a cadre of educated Cherokees. A few years later, the Cherokee embarked on an ambitious kindergarten-through-college educational system in English and Cherokee. It was the first bilingual and bicultural school system in the nation. Judging by today's standards, the system was amazing, with evidence that it produced a 90 percent literate population within a decade. Even today, that record cannot be matched by most states. In spite of Indian removal in 1830 the schools continued to develop and grow in Indian Territory. By the end of the nineteenth century, most Cherokee were literate, better educated than their white neighbors, and in control of their destiny.[2]

This control was short-lived, however. The federal government, opposed the concept of 'cultural pluralism' as a threat to nationhood. Assimilating immigrants through the public school system, was (to their mind) the key factor in producing national and individual social and economic progress. They saw cultural pluralism as a barrier to assimilation. Comparing the success of immigrants to the failure of Indians to assimilate had an obvious logical flaw. The immigrants chose to come to this country and chose to integrate, while the Indians were in their own country and chose to remain Indian.

One advocate of Americanizing Indians was Colonel Henry Pratt. He had fought both in the Civil and in the Indian wars. In 1879 Pratt petitioned Washington for old army barracks used during the Civil War in Carlisle, Pennsylvania, and turned this site into the first off-reservation boarding school for Indian youth. His plea in Congress was to "immerse the Indians in waters of our civilization and when we get them under water, hold them there until they are thoroughly soaked" which he admitted would "eradicate the Indian but make the man." He had strong support in Congress.[3]

From then on, Congress, impatient to Americanize Indians, appropriated money to build 106 off-reservation boarding schools between 1879 and the early 1900s. In 1892, Congress authorized the BIA to withhold rations from any Indian family unwilling to have their child sent away to school. Education, Congress agreed, should inculcate Indian assimilation into mainstream society. Coercion was used to remove children from the home and keep them in boarding schools from the ages of six to sixteen. Indians no longer had the option, as the Virginia chiefs once had, to refuse to send their children to non-Indian schools.

In 1906, Congress abolished the Oklahoma Cherokee tribal school system. Dissolving the system led to social, economic, and political devastation for this tribe. From a 90 percent literacy rate in the nineteenth century, tribe members plummeted to an average of 5.3 years of schooling in 1968, meaning more than half of the tribe was functionally illiterate within seven decades of federal/state control of Cherokee education.[4]

A tribe that once produced the manpower necessary to operate its own social, economic, and political institutions, was reduced to colonial supervision by the Bureau of Indian Affairs. The foreboding of the old chiefs in Virginia bore fruit. The students in these boarding schools were ill-equipped to contribute to Indian or non-Indian society. They were in fact "good for nothing." To solidify white domination completely, even Cherokee leadership was selected by the president of the United States and not by general election of the Cherokee. In the 1970s, for the first time in this century, the Cherokee were allowed to run their own elections for tribal leaders.

This tribe, one of many who experienced similar patterns of social policy, is an example of how the institution of education was designed to perpetuate the colonial ethic. At the same time, the Cherokee example provides insight into reasons Indians have been less than enthusiastic about non-Indian education.

There are other reasons as well, which have to do with the concept of 'racial inferiority.' There was a widely held belief that the size of the head was a measurement of the brain, and, consequently, the capacity to think. In any effort to prove his theory, after the Indian wars, a doctor from the Smithsonian Institution wrote letters to army personnel in the field requesting skeletons of Indians so he could measure their skulls. More than 18,500 skeletons were collected by that museum alone. These remains are still in the basement of the Smithsonian. Not to be outdone, Harvard collected about 5,000 specimens, and the National Park Service has about 20,000 stashed away at various sites.

The concept of Indian racial inferiority attained credence with a publication by Lewis Terman (Stanford University) in 1916 that stated that certain racial types would benefit from education minimally at best. Terman was one half of the team that created the Stanford Binet (IQ) test. He wrote:

> Their dullness seems to be racial, or at least inherent in the family stock from which they come. The fact that one meets this type with such extraordinary frequency among Indians, Mexicans and Negroes suggests quite forcibly that the whole question of racial differences in mental traits will have to be taken up anew . . . there will be discovered enormously significant racial differences . . . which cannot be wiped out of any schemes of mental culture.
>
> Children of this group should be segregated in special classes . . . they cannot master abstractions, but they can often be made efficient workers.[5]

Indians were reputed to be racially inferior. This presumption of inferiority was widely held by the public and concomitantly, in the public school systems. Some states even enacted ordinances forbidding enrollment of minorities, including Indians. An example of this attitude was California's Political Code Section 662 (1924): "The governing body of the school districts shall have power to exclude children of filthy or vicious habits, or children suffering from contagious or infectious diseases, and also to establish separate schools for Indian children, and for children of Chinese, Japanese or Mongolian parentage"

Congress thought the assimilation process could be speeded up by enrolling Indian children in the public schools. They knew there was public resistance to this move, and to overcome objections, passed the Snyder Act in 1921.

This act authorized the Bureau of Indian Affairs to establish and fund educational programs that benefit Indians. Included in Snyder was a provision to subsidize public schools that enrolled Indian students.

The western states especially, with large Indian populations, took the position that Indian education was a federal responsibility. Tribal lands could not be taxed, and Indians were not citizens of the United States. Congress attacked the citizenship barrier with the passage of the Indian Citizenship Act in 1924. Proponents of public education pointed out that public schools enroll children whose parents do not own property, or who are unemployed.

The Bureau of Indian Affairs was under attack from all sides. Reports from the philanthropic Committee of One Hundred, followed by the Brookings Institution Meriam Report and congressional field studies led to the inescapable conclusion that Indian education administered by the BIA was a failure.

The first to openly attack the Bureau of Indian Affairs education system was the Committee of One Hundred in 1923. The Committee of One Hundred was a select group of reputable intellectuals and philanthropists dedicated to Indian affairs. Because of the influence of its members, the publication of the committee's report produced public clamor for profound changes in Indian education policy. Although widely circulated, the bureau largely ignored this report. The impact, however, led to a congressional investigation in 1928, which was conducted on reservations throughout the country.

The thirty-volume 1928 congressional report, *Survey of the Conditions of the Indians of the United States,* concluded that the Indian service education system was disastrous and there was evidence of corruption within the BIA. Under siege from all directions, Secretary of the Interior Hubert Work requested the Brookings Institution to conduct a thorough study of the BIA. Heading up this study was Dr. Lewis Meriam. If Work had hoped that an independent nongovernmental report would be less vitriolic than the report given by the Committee of One Hundred and/or the 1928 congressional hearings, he must have been sadly disappointed.

The Meriam Report

Meriam contracted with Dr. W. Carson Ryan of Swarthmore to conduct the education segment of the report. Ryan's credentials to conduct this study were outstanding. As Margaret Szasz observed:

Ryan was a nationally known educator. He had worked for the U.S. Bureau of Education from 1912 to 1920. In 1918 he had received his doctorate from George Washington University. Shortly thereafter he had served for a year as educational editor for the New York Evening Post. Although he had been appointed professor of education at Swarthmore in 1921, this had not curtailed a broad use of his talents. By the time Ryan began work on the Meriam Report he was already recognized as an expert in educational surveys. Between 1917 and 1929 he conducted seven studies of education systems from Saskatchewan, Canada, to the Virgin Islands, including American Indian education (1926–27). At the same time he had served as American delegate to several international education meetings.[6]

Ryan was a proponent of a new concept in education, known as "progressive education," whose guru was John Dewey. The basic belief of progressive education was to integrate education with experience. The home, the neighborhood, and the student's culture were all to be used in the process of education. To be sure, Dewey had in mind the swarms of immigrant children living in city slums when he wrote:

Perhaps the greatest of all pedagogical fallacies is the notion that a person learns only the particular thing he is studying at the time. Collateral learning in the way of formation of enduring attitudes, of likes and dislikes, may be and often is much more important than the spelling lesson or lessons in geography or history that is learned. For these attitudes are fundamentally what count in the future. The most important attitude that can be formed is that of desire to go on learning. If impetus in this direction is weakened instead of being intensified, sometimes much more than mere lack of preparation takes place. The pupil is actually robbed of native capacities which otherwise would enable him to cope with the circumstances that he meets in the course of his life. We often see persons who have had little schooling and in whose case the absence of set schooling proves to be a positive asset. They have at least retained their native common sense and power of judgment, and their exercise in the actual conditions of living has given them the precious gift of ability to learn from the experiences they have. *What avail is it to win prescribed amounts of information about geography and history, to win ability to read and write, if in the process the individual loses his own soul*: loses his appreciation of things worth while, of the values to which these things are relative; if he loses desire to apply what he had learned, and above all, loses the ability to extract meaning from his future experiences as they occur? (my emphasis)[7]

Ryan's personal philosophy of education was influenced by Dewey but also evolved because of his own observation that public education systems were two-tiered, one for the children of the elite and middle class, the other for the poor and off-spring of immigrants.

He observed that education for the poor and/or immigrant youngster had as its main objective the obliteration of immigrant native language, custom, and culture and integration of the "American" language, holidays, heroes, culture and values. They were taught by rote learning. Ryan observed the objective of public education for the masses (albeit poor and/or first-generation immigrants) was to produce efficient workers for a rapidly expanding industrial economy. Success was measured by the numbers of students who entered the work force in factories and positions of manual labor.

However, he observed, the children of the middle class/wealthy attended public/private schools where critical thinking provided the necessary training for college and professional preparation. The standard by which these schools were evaluated was the number of graduates who later became professionals in the nation's political, social, and economic institutions.

Ryan concluded that Indian education followed the same pattern Dewey had found in the city slum schools for immigrant children:

> The most fundamental need in Indian education is a change in point of view. Whatever may have been the official governmental attitude, education for the Indian in the past has proceeded largely on the theory that it is necessary to remove the Indian child as far as possible from his home environment; whereas the modern point of view in education and social work lays stress on upbringing in the natural setting of home and family life.[8]

Ryan was particularly critical of the teaching staff in the Indian schools.

> After all is said that can be said, about the skill and devotion of some employees, the fact remains that the government of the United States regularly takes into the instructional staff of its Indian schools teachers whose credentials would not be accepted in good public school systems, and into the institutional side of these schools key employees—matrons and the like—who could not meet the standards set up by modern social agencies.[9]

Distasteful to Ryan was the federal policy of uprooting Indian children from their homes and sending them to schools far away from home. He found that they had no opportunity to see their families for years at a time. If they ran away, the army or Indian service picked them up and took them back to school. If families hid their children from these officials, family rations were withheld until the child was delivered to a BIA official.

Ryan was especially outraged by the inhumane conditions the children were subjected to in the Indian schools. He found that the children "were being fed on 11 cents a day," which was seriously undermining their health. He found tuberculosis to be widespread and malnutrition endemic in the Indian schools.

The most serious charge Ryan leveled at the BIA was that learning played a secondary role throughout the system. Of primary importance was the child labor force which was used to a large extent to support the school. Half of the day was spent working in the school, and the other half in class time. Ryan argued that children need to experience full-time education. What was worse, he observed:

> If the labor of the boarding school is to be done by the pupils, it is essential that the pupils be old enough and strong enough to do institutional work. In nearly every boarding school one will find children of 10, 11, and 12 spending four hours a day in more or less heavy industrial work—dairying, kitchen work, laundry and shop. The work is bad for children of this age, especially children not physically well-nourished; most of it in no sense educational, since the operations are large scale and bear little relation to either home or industrial life outside.[10]

As the expression goes, "If you're not part of the solution, you are part of the problem." Ryan set out to become part of the solution. After writing his report, he accepted the position of director of education for the Bureau of Indian Affairs. In spite of his own criticism of off-reservation boarding schools, as director of education, Ryan held onto them as a less odious alternative to bussing students hours daily to the nearest school. (Some roads were impassable during inclement weather, and many reservations had rudimentary and often hazardous dirt roads.)

The crux of Ryan's reform policy was the development of cross-cultural curriculum within the off-reservation boarding schools. At the same time, he aggressively sought appropriations for the building and maintenance of day schools. Ryan saw day and/or boarding schools as intermediate solutions to Indian education. He was confident that public education was the ultimate solution to the Indian problem. He believed assimilation was a necessary societal objective, but it could and should be accomplished in more humane ways.

Fortunately for Ryan, in 1933 John Collier replaced Charles J. Rhoads as the new "reform" commissioner of Indian affairs. Collier not only became his staunch ally, but was, like Ryan, a passionate and idealistic champion of Indian rights.

Collier was a young social worker from New York who became interested in Indian affairs after visiting New Mexico. In New Mexico, he learned about the Bursam Bill proposed by Senator Bursum of New Mexico in 1928. This bill proposed to make available for homesteading unclaimed land, that is, land not backed up by a deed or grant. Some anthropologists claim that the present pueblos were built at least one thousand years ago, so the concept of having a "deed" or land grant was ludicrous. Collier's fight against the Bursam Bill united Indian Country in support of his appointment as the new commissioner of Indian affairs.

In the reform fever of the era, Collier was able to get the Indian Reorganization Act and the Johnson O'Malley Act (JOM) passed through Congress in 1934. JOM authorized contractual agreements with states (among other entities) to pay for the education of Indian children in the public school system. Federal education policy shifted from sending Indian children to off-reservation boarding schools to public schools.

The Johnson O'Malley Act

The Meriam report recommended education of Indian children in public schools was the ultimate solution to the Indian education problem. Ryan knew that some reservations were too large and too far removed from public schools. However, where it was feasible, he pushed for Indian children to attend public schools as a means of providing better education. He personally believed children were naturally flexible and better adjusted to American society when they attended integrated schools. Collier agreed and lobbied Congress for the JOM Act.

Initially, the BIA attempted to monitor the use of JOM funds to ensure that Indian children were receiving the education and the services necessary for successful integration into the public system. But when schools balked at federal intrusion upon what they considered their domain, rather than withdraw funds or change policy, the BIA relied upon the states to monitor and local communities to adhere to, the intent and spirit of the law. In fact, two years later, the JOM Act was amended to provide federal subsidies not only to states, but also to "political subdivisions, or with any State university, college or school, or with any appropriate state or private corporation, agency or institution for the education, medical attention, agricultural assistance and social welfare, including relief of distress of Indians in such state or Territory, through the agencies of the state or Territory.[11]

Collier and Ryan were an interesting combination of pragmatists and idealists. Politically both understood that state (particularly western states) opposition to federal monitoring would eventuate in political lobbying in Congress, with the high probability that the JOM Act would be amended. As pragmatists, they permitted (and hoped) each state receiving JOM funding would assume responsibility for monitoring these funds. Their idealism was a blind spot, because they could not perceive of public school districts misusing federal Indian education funds. This problem came to light decades later, when evaluations were conducted on the use of federal Indian education funds in public schools.

Collier and Ryan felt their energy could best be used by concentrating on developing school curriculum and cross-cultural teacher training in Indian service schools.

The blind faith Collier and Ryan had in the integrity of public education was not shared by Indian communities. It took a little more than three decades for their complaints to be heard, but finally, in 1971, a national study was conducted on JOM and Indian education.

That year, the NAACP Legal Defense and Educational Funds and the Center for Law and Education at Harvard University combined efforts to study the effects of public education on Indian children. *An Even Chance* remains to this day the most systematic analysis of public education for Indian children. Comprehensive in scope, the report field evaluated ten school districts in Arizona with an Indian enrollment of 14,431; eight school districts in Montana with an Indian enrollment of 5,015; eleven school districts in North Dakota with an Indian enrollment of 1,523; eight school districts in New Mexico with an Indian enrollment of 19,742; one school district in New York with an Indian enrollment of 5,710; six school districts in Oklahoma with an Indian enrollment of 24,003; two school districts in Oregon with an Indian enrollment of 3,601; sixteen school districts in South Dakota with an Indian enrollment of 16,533.[12]

An Even Chance reported that JOM funds amounted to 19.6 million in 1971. They traced the funds from the federal government to the different states and, ultimately, to local school districts. They found that the states did not monitor the use of JOM funds: "In almost every district, even if the state did not use JOM for general support, school superintendents told us that JOM funds were combined with the school system's general fund and they could not account for how the money was spent."[13]

School districts used JOM funds to reduce local taxes for education. "As a result Federal funds received by school systems based on Indian enrollment and intended to benefit Indian children, are used, at least in part, to maintain a reduced financial effort on the part of local property owners."[14]

JOM was intended to help Indian parents meet the cost of education by providing funds for school lunches, athletic equipment, books, school supplies and graduation fees: "School districts in Arizona, the report said, "do not use JOM funds for parental costs . . . Our interviewers in the Navajo Nation reported that many Indian students simply dropout of school because they cannot pay their fees or buy supplies. No school officials bothered to tell them they are entitled to federal dollars to meet these needs."[15] They documented the Grants, New Mexico, school district federal reimbursement for physical education equipment for Indian children, course fees, and gym shoes, none of which the students received. Worse yet, Indian students were told if they did not pay their school fees, they would not receive their grades.

Federal support under JOM provided for school lunches because many Indian families were living at or below poverty level. The report observed that in school district after school district, the children were made to feel the stigma of accepting a free lunch. Some districts, such as Tuba City, required a daily assertion of poverty in order to get lunch. In Page, Arizona, Indian parents had to sign a statement each month indicating that they did not have money for their children's lunch bills. In Madras, Oregon, Indian children were charged for their lunches and had to pay in advance. In Parshall, North Dakota, JOM students were separated in the lunch line.

Another provision of JOM provided funds for "special projects" which was to meet the special education needs of Indian children. *An Even Chance* reported school districts used the funds to benefit all children, not just Indian children. For instance, the study found that the

> Dupree Independent School District in South Dakota received funds for the purchase of mobiles. They argued that this purchase was necessary in order to be able to handle its present enrollment of 257 students but the district only had 89 Indian children enrolled. . . . In Los Lunas School District in New Mex-

ico a kindergarten was financed out of JOM funds, but only a handful of Indian children were enrolled. In another school district, Indian children were using torn and tattered school books even though funds were allocated for school books and materials.[16]

Virtually all Indian communities wanted tribal history, language, and culture taught in the schools, but the survey found school officials "did not recognize this as a need,": "Curricula and materials used in the public schools do not include Indian culture studies. Neither are they provided as a general policy by special federal programs for Indian children in the public schools. Yet, ethnic studies were given a high priority by all the parents we interviewed."

The report confirmed what Indian communities knew all along: school districts were using JOM funds illegally and circumventing the spirit and intent of the law. That in itself would not have mobilized their anger. The hue and cry came as a result of the Coleman Report and the Kennedy hearings that confirmed calamitous drop-out rates of Indian children even in grammar school. A study conducted by the Northwest Regional Educational Laboratory in 1968 reported that Indian students were dropping out of high schools in some districts at rates as low as 50 percent and as high as 85 percent. *An Even Chance* conducted a study of another public-school entitlement funding, generally referred to as "Impact Aid."

Impact Aid

Impact Aid (P.L. 81–874 and P.L.81–815) was enacted with the start of the Korean War in 1950. Because of the military build-up and troop movements from state to state, Congress sought to relieve local school districts from the financial burden of educating children of armed-service personnel. Increasingly aware of the need for social programs and a department to administer these programs, Congress created the Department of Health, Education, and Welfare (DHEW) in 1953. This agency administered Impact Aid to the nation's school districts.

By 1958, Impact Aid entitlements to local school districts was amended to include Indian children living on or near federal (albeit reservation) lands. In addition to JOM, local public schools with Indian enrollments had dual sources of federal funding; one administered by the BIA, the other by the DHEW. Congress was aware of dual funding but felt that JOM might fund the services Indian students required, while Impact Aid would support normal operating services as a result of increased student population. Impact Aid, or 81–874, to support school expenses accompanied 81–815 to support the cost of new buildings and equipment necessary to accommodate larger student populations. Construction expenditures are awarded on a competitive basis, and even when projects are approved, it takes years and sometimes as long as a decade for funding to be approved. The law was amended in 1970 to give Indian schools equal priority with other requests.

The Even Chance research team set out to study whether this new bureaucracy (DHEW) was any better than the Bureau of Indian Affairs at monitoring Indian education entitlements to public schools. In 1969, the year of the Impact Aid study, $27.9 million was earmarked for school districts with Indian student enrollment. The funding formula is based upon the expenditures each district allocates for students from local taxes and the average daily attendance of Indian students.

The report of the Gallup, New Mexico, county public school found that

the inferior and substandard education which Indian children receive in districts such as Gallup is especially galling because Indian children bring in more money per child than non-Indians. DHEW, sent the average of $306.70 per Indian child for the year 1970, $153.35 for the child of a federal employee to local school districts. This contrasted sharply with an average of $127.00 the local school district provided for their own children through property taxes. Of all the districts we surveyed, the GALLUP-McKINLEY COUNTY SCHOOL DISTRICT in New Mexico (a predominantly Indian district with a total enrollment of 12,000) provides the clearest example of inequalities between schools. The difference between predominantly Indian schools and predominantly non-Indian schools is great. For example, the Indian Hills Elementary School which has an enrollment of 294 of which only one-third is Indian is located in a middle-income area of the town of Gallup. The school has a split level, carpeted music room, a carpeted library; uncrowded and well-equipped classroom, a gymnasium and a separate cafeteria. There are plenty of showers, toilets and drinking fountains. There is a paved courtyard. The school has closed-circuit TV. Although Indian Hills Elementary is not a title I target school, our interviewers found Title I equipment there. Five miles away from Indian Hills School is the Church Rock Elementary School with a 97% Navajo enrollment. The school is a barrack-like structure, surrounded by mounds of sand that drift in through cracks in doors and windows. The "all purpose" assembly hall serves as cafeteria, gymnasium and assembly hall. There are four temporary classrooms which have no extra sanitary facilities. The classrooms are dark and crowded, the furniture worn and old.[17]

In addition to the above sources of funding, public schools apply for and receive funding under Title 1 (for educationally disadvantaged children) and Title 5 (formerly Title 4), the Indian Education Act, part A (formula) and part B (discretionary). All of the above are currently administered by the U.S. Department of Education.

Since the Collier regime, more Indian children have attended public schools than Indian schools. It was touted as the solution to achieving educational equity with white children in the public systems. The truth is that we shall never know whether this policy might have been the solution. We know that without diligent monitoring, school systems simply took the money and ran.

An Even Chance reported:

The Office of Education which administers the Impact Aid legislation takes the position that the Federal government is not in the business of investigating the "suitability" of public education, which is considered the responsibility of the state and local government. Nor does the Federal government determine whether Impact Aid pupils, including Indians, are receiving their fair share of the congressional appropriations.[18]

In 1954, the U.S. Supreme Court ruled in the famous *Brown vs. Topeka* case. The federal government found itself in the uncomfortable role of monitoring state and local education agencies to guarantee equal educational opportunities for black children. The obligation to monitor educational equity with respect to black children made it untenable to continue a laissez faire policy regarding Indian students. By the sixties, Indians found strong and vocal support from social scientists and educators. The Coleman report in 1966 took direct aim at the public school system and was particularly instrumental in the creation of the Kennedy hearings of 1968.

The Coleman Report

In 1966, James Coleman conducted a national study on the effectiveness of public-school education for minorities entitled *Equality of Educational Opportunity.* The target population of this study coming on the heels of the civil rights movement and *Brown vs. Topeka,* was black students, but Coleman also examined the effects of public education on American Indian children. He reported Indian children were achieving less than black children in the public-school systems. His findings are even more compelling when measured against the federal funds available to public schools for the education of Indian children, not otherwise available for the education of other minorities: "Of all the different minority groups, Coleman reported, it is the American Indian whose verbal and national average reading scores show a large decrease in relative standing over the grades, which shows the training they receive does not allow them to maintain the relative standing among other groups with which they began school."[19]

In other words, the longer an Indian child stayed in school, the greater the age/grade gap widened. Coleman's study found that Indian high-school seniors were performing on an age/grade level of first-year high-school students. Federal Indian education subsidies motivated public schools to retain Indian children (although there was a high drop-out rate) but not necessarily to educate them effectively.

The Kennedy Report

In 1968 Robert Kennedy, and later his brother Edward, chaired congressional hearings on Indian education. Much of the same criticism leveled at the Bureau of Indian Affairs in the Meriam report forty years earlier was repeated in the Kennedy report. The only difference was the focus of public rather than Indian service education. The report found that despite substantial federal funding, the highest dropout rate of any group in the country was by the American Indian.

At Kennedy's encouragement Indians from all over the county testified before Congress. Many Indians had to pay their own way since few tribal councils could afford to help them. Yet they came, and they stayed in the cheapest hotel rooms our nation's capital has to offer. Nothing deterred them from having their say before

Congress. Tribe after tribe aired complaints before a shocked and bewildered congressional committee.

The anecdotal Indian testimony during the Kennedy hearings was substantially corroborated by the National Regional Educational Laboratory comprehensive study *The American Indian High School Dropout—The Magnitude of the Problem*. This study was compelling because it was longitudinal, following the same Indian students over years and from school to school. As they explained: "This study has differed from other dropout studies in that the students registered in the same grade on a specific date who constituted the target population were each identified by name. The progress through school of each student was then traced to high school graduate or another specific date almost five years later unless death or dropout from school occurred prior to that time."[20]

The study of students in grades eight through twelve concentrated on the Indian student populations in public schools (and some BIA-operated schools) in the states of Oregon, Washington, Idaho, and North and South Dakota. The study revealed the average dropout rate of Indian students at grade 8 was about 50 percent. South Dakota had the highest drop-out rate of 85 percent. The school districts studied by the National Regional Educational Laboratory received federal Indian education entitlements to provide basic and special-education needs. The BIA-operated schools were funded through congressional appropriations. In spite of the money that went into solving the problem, the problems not only persisted, but were more severe than when Ryan conducted the Meriam report study.

In essence, the reforms of Collier and Ryan and the attempts to integrate Indians into public education had failed. The failure is directly attributable to placing Indian education funds outside of the scrutiny of the Indian communities, rendering Indians powerless to direct effective education for their young. Collier and Ryan, both idealists and innovative educators, could not conceive Indians as the solution to creating an educational milieu to achieve excellence. At the same time, they failed to incorporate reasonable federal monitoring procedures within the funding process. The schools were not held accountable either by the Indians or by the federal agencies. In effect, the lack of provisions to hold public schools accountable undermined the intent and spirit of Indian education funding.

Tribal aspirations to operate their own schools as they had in the last century came alive again through Johnson's War on Poverty. President Johnson created a new agency for social change, the Office of Economic Opportunity, (OEO). The OEO was an agency that took risks with an uncompromising understanding that poor people, if given opportunity, could make positive and productive changes in their lives. In Indian Country, OEO developed guidelines providing the possibility of Indian-controlled schools. OEO's first experiment in 1966 was Rough Rock Demonstration School on the Navajo reservation.

The funding of Indian programs by OEO challenged the exclusive autonomy once held by the Department of Education and the Bureau of Indian Affairs. Both these agencies took their complaints to Congress during the Kennedy hearings. They testified that OEO-funded schools were being administered by Indian amateurs and had a deleterious effect on Indian education.

Madison Coombs was deputy director of education when Rough Rock, financed by OEO, began operations. During the Kennedy hearings, he openly criticized Rough Rock and Navajo methodology. He concluded that they "have furnished clear evidence that control and not the quality of education is the significant goal of the sponsors."[21]

In her book, *Education and the American Indian,* Margaret Szasz cites an article written by Coombs, "The Indian Child Goes to School," in which he claims that a comparative study showed that Indian children tested higher in public schools than those who attended federal and mission schools. His statements contradicted the study published by the Northwest Regional Educational Laboratory (1968) which found an extraordinarily high dropout rate of Indians in public schools (50 to 85 percent) and the findings of *An Even Chance* in 1971.

Those (federal Indian money) dollars have been used for every conceivable school system need except the need that Congress had in mind. Impact Aid and Johnson O'Malley dollars support general operating expenses of local school districts and thus make it possible for those districts to reduce taxes for non-Indian property owners. Special programs, which should serve Indian needs, in fact serve the total school population. Title I and Johnson O'Malley dollars purchase system-wide services. Those dollars pay for teachers' aids who serve all the children, not the educationally deprived Indian children. They buy fancy equipment for every child, not just the eligible Indian children. They provide kindergarten classes for all children, not just the eligible children. They buy mobile classrooms which become permanent facilities for all students. In sum, Indians do not get the educational benefits that they are, by law, entitled to receive.[22]

In spite of the self-serving testimony of administrators from the BIA and the Department of Education, the overwhelming evidence produced during the Kennedy hearings supported the contention that both agencies had failed to produce an educated Indian population. Congress was in no mood for excuses and once again, went back to the drawing board.

If the Indian service failed to educate the Indian child, if the public schools performed equally miserably, then the solution to Indian educational achievement must lie somewhere else. One inescapable solution was to legislate vigorous parental input as a requisite for states and public schools to receive Indian education funds.

Change in the abysmal educational attainment of Indian children logically demanded that Indian parents and tribes would have to be a part of the solution. Recognizing that which had escaped Collier and so many before and after him, Congress passed the Indian Education Act in 1972, with provisions for Indian parents/ and/or tribal participation within the school systems. This was followed by the Indian Self-Determination Act of 1975 (93–638). Under provisions of both these acts, tribes and tribal Indian organizations can operate their own schools and programs formerly operated by the Bureau of Indian Affairs. It has since been amended to give even greater strength to tribal autonomy.

Tribal autonomy conflicts sharply with the ideas of melting-pot theorists and policy makers. The greater the independence, tribal education asserts, the wider the chasm between the goals of assimilationists and the goals of tribal self-determination. It should be a surprise to no one that Indian control has many critics among government policy makers. They had envisioned that the goals of tribes would correspond or at least harmonize with the national educational goals.

But, as pointed out earlier, education is a political act, an institution that is designed for nation-building. The best interests of tribal nations are not necessarily the best interests of the United States, and to measure tribal education in terms of public or BIA education, which is essentially an assimilationist or colonial model, is to deny the right of tribes to design education to meet their national goals.

Just as public education is a political act, the process of evaluation is equally political. By definition, evaluations measure the intent of education using content (a commonly agreed-upon body of knowledge) as its yardstick. For instance, when the chiefs of various tribes in Virginia (mentioned earlier) assessed the education of some of their young Indians at a colonial college, they used the yardstick of how competent the graduates were in terms of living in the woods, hunt successfully, speak Indian fluently, and contribute to the tribe. However, the elite of Virginia assessed success in terms of how well the Indian students spoke English, learned the Christian Bible, dressed similarly with their colonial colleagues, and were able to integrate into colonial society. While the former did not mind that their students learned English and colonial ways, they were dismayed that these were to the exclusion of tribal education. They were in fact embracing a multicultural model, but the latter assumed an assimilationist (or later what would be termed "melting-pot") model.

Little has changed from those early days. There is no disagreement that the assimilationist and cultural pluralistic models are interested in assessing Indian student achievement in reading, comprehension, math, and science. After that, the two models of evaluative inquiry diverge sharply. Assimilationist evaluations focus exclusively on the acquisition of knowledge while the cultural pluralistic model goes beyond the statistics with an investigation of the fit between culture and education. This is the model usually endorsed by Indian educators because, unlike European immigrants who permitted the institution of education to trade their cultural/historical past for an economically mobile future for their children, the Indian race sought a future without relinquishing their past or their culture for their children.

One other aspect needs discussion. It is highly unlikely that those early eighteenth-century Indian students graduating from the college in Virginia were integrated into either tribal or colonial society because of endemic racism in even early American society. Those early experiments in education became what sociologists term, "marginal men" existing on the periphery of American and/or tribal society. This problem exists even today, in the twentieth century. Statistics on Indian student achievement disregard the historic documentation of the effects of racism on Indian student retention, the social, political, and economic impact of Indian drop-out rates on tribal development and individual self-esteem.

This book examines two studies, the ABT study, using the colonial or melting-pot measurement of Indian student achievement, and the Madison study, measuring the cultural pluralist model.

The ABT study was commissioned to compare Indian student

achievement in tribal, BIA, and public schools in terms of cost-benefit analysis.

Evaluation of the Madison public-schools was designed from a multicultural perspective. The community in this Madison study is comparable to other communities where there are sizable Indian populations close-by or what is termed "border towns" to reservations. There are always individual differences, but on the whole, this town is similar to others in Indian Country.

To get at the heart of the Indian student-achievement enigma, one needs to understand the educational environment of these communities. The Madison illustration is a microcosm, not exact, but sufficiently extensive for the reader to understand the sociology of rural life where Indian and non-Indian meet, work, live, and die. There are no heroes. There are no villains. There are two distinct cultures who are still fighting the wars of the 1800s. It is not open warfare. No guns are used. No one openly challenges and insults another, but it is war, nonetheless. The battleground is the classroom, and the war is about the minds and the hearts of children.

As a nation, we profess belief in cultural pluralism and respect for differences. At the same time, we call ourselves the "melting pot." These two concepts are contradictory and are at the source of conflict in Indian education. Pluralism generates the John Colliers and the Indian Education and Self Determination Act. The melting pot creates the Dawes allotment and termination policies. If Indian country is confused, it is because they operate on the principle of cultural pluralism, while the educational bureaucracy fosters the melting pot.

The reality is that this nation organizes its time, money, ambitions, and classrooms to legitimize only one language, culture, religion, history, and ideal. In this tug of war, no one wins. The losers are children, all children.

2

Different Scales for Different Whales

The title of this chapter comes from an old Office of Economic Opportunity (OEO) slogan I learned as an OEO intern:

> Different strokes for different folks
> Different ways on different days
> Different scales for different whales

OEO was one of the War on Poverty programs set up during the Johnson era. This agency learned from the onset that working with, planning with, and evaluating poverty programs required flexibility and creativity since many programs targeted poor minority rural and inner-city populations, and the OEO professionals working with these groups were white, educated, and middle to upper class. The gap between class and caste could be bridged by approaching different cultures holistically. This approach appears to have lost favor with contemporary professional evaluators.

The American Indian is a "different whale" because Indian cultures have a distinctive history and culture. Indian culture is woven into a holistic tapestry of history, geography, religion, political science and sociology and does not lend itself to linear judgment. However, most evaluators are graduates trained within recognized academic spheres. Even armed with some knowledge about Indian culture it is often outside of their scope to draft a multidisciplinary evaluation plan.

The multidisciplinary approach used by the Madison evaluation team was significantly different from the methodology used by

ABT. A discussion of methodology follows a discussion of the rural schools where the evaluations took place.[1]

Rural schools are not publicly perceived as having critical educational problems because they have not received much attention from media and researchers, yet one-third of the nation's school districts (12,000) serve rural school children. It is true that these schools share characteristics with their urban brethren, in that college textbooks, teaching methodology, and licensing standards are for the most part the same whether a potential teacher trains in Boston or in Bozeman. That factor aside, rural schools have unique characteristics. The following is a brief profile of rural schools in general; rural schools with sizable Indian student enrollment, and tribal schools, which by definition are rural since most reservations are geographicaly rural.

Characteristics of Rural Schools

There is extensive evidence in the educational literature that academic excellence correlates with positive, active community and parental involvement. There are as many ways to encourage community and parental involvement as there are to discourage them. There is strong evidence that the size of the school, and the rural quality of life in the school district plays only a minor role in achieving academic excellence. In fact, a study of the rural schools in Alaska states: "The size of the high school does not determine the quality of the students' educational experience."[2] The report found other school characteristics far more significant in determining educational excellence. These are

1. A strong partnership between teachers and the community.

2. Agreement between teachers and the community on a theme for the education program.

3. An enterprising teaching staff.

4. A central office that encourages local professionals and the community to take the initiative in adapting schools to local needs.[3]

The strengths inherent in rural school systems include (but are not limited to) a close relationship between teachers and students; the likelihood that students become involved in extra-curricular activities encouraging a holistic approach to education; and a minimal bureaucratic system making it more efficient to effect policy or academic changes within reasonable time constraints.[4]

The factor which contributes most to achieving excellence is the total involvement of the community in the inner workings of the school and the utilization of school facilities for adult community activities. Both of these activities encourage community dialogue which significantly contributes to consensus and action.[5]

There are some liabilities that virtually all rural systems have in common. Among them are limited numbers of teachers, courses, and activities; limitations on specialized vocational education programs; limitations on courses for college preparation; low achievement-test scores; limited exposure to nonrural life, making transitions to college life more difficult for rural students; and excessively high teacher and administrative turn-over rates.

The overriding contributing factor in achieving academic excellence is a community's will to be excellent. Determined communities set aside parochial differences and work collectively and collaboratively to achieve a common goal. One interesting aspect of this collaborative effort is a resurgence of creative strategies unique to each community that appears to arise almost organically to involve everyone in the process of reform. Geography, the demographics of a school district, and the history of its people play major roles in the development of reform strategy. In spite of considerable liabilities rural schools have perhaps an even greater potential than urban or inner-city schools to envision and implement programs that advance excellence in education.

Characteristics of Rural Public Schools with Large Indian Enrollment

Public schools have been around for a hundred and fifty years, but only since 1934 have they been federally subsidized to educate Indian children. The addition of Impact Aid and the Indian Education Act entitlements (see the previous chapter) have added to the general support of Indian children in public schools. Although inner-city and suburban schools are entitled to these funds, because of the sheer volume of Indian students attending individual rural public schools adjacent to Indian reservations, these schools receive the bulk of the money allocated by Congress each year.

Rural schools with sizable Indian student populations have many of the strengths and weaknesses of rural schools discussed above, but because they receive substantial federal Indian education subsidies, one would assume they would allocate some of these funds to include the Indian presence in curriculum and teaching. Sadly, this is not true. As is the case with other minorities, the Indian teacher is likely to be the last hired and the first fired.

The National Coalition of Advocates for Students 1983 survey found that "many school systems are unable or unwilling to implement affirmative action policies that would diversify the teaching and administrative staff, including persons more representative of the racial and cultural minorities served by the schools. As a school desegregation officer said in Boston 'we must have multicultural models in the schools if we are to shatter the myth of minority inferiority and white superiority.' "[6]

When an Indian child goes to a public school he/she observes that there are no Indian teachers. In rural public schools adjacent to reservations, Indian children can not help but be impressed with the fact that the cook, bus driver, and cleaning person are Indians. These visual impressions persuade Indian children to infer that Indian is inferior and white is superior, because all the positions of knowledge and power lie within the white staff, while all the service people are Indian.

As they advance in grade, they learn French or German and about France and Germany, but not about Indian language or Indian culture: "This lack of respect, along with a disregard for the students' languages and cultures in many schools enrolling Indian students both on and off reservations are contributing to the disappearance of tribal languages and identity. At the same time, they are having a devastating effect on school achievement and retention. To continue to ignore such issues is not acceptable."[7]

For many students living near Indian reservations, there is no sound educational basis for inclusion of French, German, or Spanish to the exclusion of Indian languages, especially since Indian linguists would be more readily available from the surrounding reservations. There are as many non-Indians as Indians who would like to study Indian languages precisely because it would facilitate communication between the two neighboring races.

These attitudinal factors (the exclusion of relevant Indian subject matter and Indian professionals) contribute significantly to the abysmal dropout rate of Indian students.

"Some counselors have discouraged Indian children from either staying in school or returning to school after dropping out . . . some teachers are not sensitive enough, in dealing with the understanding of the Indian culture, and convey the message, either knowingly or unknowing, that Indian children do not belong in the classroom and have little concern over their attendance and school work."[8]

A considerable number of (but not all) rural schools with sizable Indian populations and funding exclude the Indian presence in professional roles, curriculum, and programs.

Characteristics of Indian-Controlled Schools

If it is possible to pinpoint the impetus for the resurgence of tribal schools, it was probably during the Kennedy congressional hearings in 1968. Although there were substantive professional assessments of public and BIA school systems, it may very well have been the parents that finally tilted the balance toward the passage of the Indian Education Act followed by the Self-Determination Act.

Indian parents testified before Congress and spoke eloquently about the damage their children were suffering at the hands of indifferent teachers and arrogant public school systems. Congress listened. They passed laws allowing tribes to open and operate their own schools.

After legislation was passed, tribal councils held community hearings to design the mission of tribal schools. Parents reiterated their contention that nothing could be achieved at the educational level without reversing the endemic low self-esteem of Indian children. Whether one believes competence breeds confidence, or confidence breeds competence, the fact is that tribal schools set out to build confidence as the foundation for competence and organized their efforts accordingly.

The profile of students attending tribal schools differs markedly from Indian students attending public or even BIA schools. Students of Indian-Controlled School (ICS) tend to have greater educational and emotional needs because they are likely to have been raised within the tribal tradition, speak Indian as a primary language, and have experienced psychological defeat in the public or BIA school systems they previously attended.

Indian schools normally hire Indian faculty when available, but there is a pervasive shortage of well-trained Indian educators to meet the needs of current tribal schools, let alone those currently in the planning stage. ICS faculty salaries have to compete with public and BIA schools and generally attract faculty who are new to the field. While Indian teachers serve as positive role models to the student body, they are also neophytes to teaching and require careful administrative supervision. Tribes have shown remarkable color blindness with non-Indian faculty who establish rapport with young Indians. They tend to be older and more experienced, requiring less supervision.

Tribal schools are young and experimental. Most began a decade ago and are still working on bilingual and bicultural curriculua and teaching methodology. Integrating tribally relevant education with standardized public school curriculua is no easy task. It takes a great deal of money and equipment. Exacerbating the problems, tribal schools are on annual appropriations, unlike public and BIA schools, posing a serious barrier to long-range planning. Most tribal school funding is designated for school operation, not research and development. Tribal schools operate in continual crisis, struggling to meet the tribal educational mission, develop innovative teaching materials, and live within the constraints of the BIA budget.

In spite of the priority placed on instilling self-esteem, Indian parents are equally adamant in exacting academic rigor from tribal schools. They hope, as do all parents, for their children to mature into productive adults, and they insist that tribal schools can achieve the dual mission of emotional support and academic excellence. They have very little patience with administrative complaints that budgetary constraints necessitate tough choices between hiring counselors, faculty, or curriculum developers. ICS schools are on the proverbial hotseat because unlike in other school bureaucracies, Indian parents have access to the governing board (the tribal council), and they are not shy about expressing their concern.

The uppermost priorities of Indian-controlled schools are self-confidence and then academic competence because of the legacy of crippling alienation Indian students experienced in other school systems. The unique educational mission of these schools, in combination with budgetary constraints and dedicated (but inexperienced) makes for a major academic challenge. These problems are not insoluble. They are simply not easily solved.

The Framework of the ABT and Madison Studies

Congress was between the proverbial rock and a hard place. On the one hand, they passed the Self-Determination Act expressly conferring the legal authority of primary and secondary Indian education to the tribes. On the other hand, both the Department of Education and the Bureau of Indian Affairs objected to the change. They complained that they were unable to get a handle on evaluating the progress Indian students were making (or not making) outside of the normal state and federal systems.[9] They alleged that each tribe setting its own standards and mission was tantamount to educational anarchy. Fiscal conservatives in Congress raised the question of whether additional expenditures allocated to Indian control schools over and above allocations to Bureau of Indian Affairs and public schools for Indian education were justifiable in the face of budget cuts?[10] All these forces provided the political impetus for regulation and/or abating the escalating growth of tribal schools.

The solution proposed by the Department of Education was a comparative research evaluation of some tribal schools. BIA schools, and public schools. This appeared to Congress a reasonable compromise. The politics of education was patently transparent when the Department of Education sent out a request for proposals (RFP) outlining the scope and framework of the evaluation process in that the public and BIA systems were not scrutinized to the same extent as the tribal schools. ABT applied and was accepted. The paramount question raised was whether quality education can be achieved in Indian-controlled schools unless they adopt instructional standards identical to those of public schools. This question was based upon the assumption that public schools have a higher standard of instruction than ICS. The underlying philosophy was the "melting-pot" supposition, that is, that the institution of education must advance assimilation in the national interest.

Consequently, although not articulated within the methodology framework, the ABT study hypothesized that the Indian student attending a public school would achieve higher academic standards at less expense than the Indian child attending an Indian-controlled school.

Around the same time, the Madison school system was being evaluated because of grievances filed by Indian parents. The complaints listed were that their children, who represented 70 percent of the student body, were being denied equal education in spite of Indian education entitlement funds largely supporting the school system. Specifically, they complained about being excluded from any meaningful role in the administration, faculty, and curriculum of the system.

The underlying philosophy of the Madison evaluation is that the best interest of the nation, both tribal and American, is that the institution of education should advance multiculturalism.

Within the framework of the Indian community complaints,

The Madison Study hypothesized that institutional racism, (the exclusion of minorities from the rewards of power, prestige and privilege) whether on a subconscious or conscious level, deprecates the intellectual capacity of Indian students and professionals and is the singular most significant factor in contributing towards the low academic achievement of Indians. Indian educators disagree on many things, but there is no disagreement on the shared memories of experiencing low teacher expectations in school. Some have survived the shredding of self-esteem, but none have forgotten. Or forgiven.

To keep a people ignorant of the most precious part of their heritage is to debilitate people.[11]

These two different premises, melting pot and multiculturalism, eventuated in two diametrically opposed evaluative methodologies. The ABT methodology statistically measured Indian student achievement, costs and attendance apart from the surrounding community. The Madison methodology measured achievement, curriculum and teaching methodology in the school, and expectations of faculty, administration, and community because it assumed the education system was a part of, not apart from, the community.

3

The ABT Study

Many tribes wasted little time after the enactment of the Self-Determination Act in establishing educational codes independent of federal or state codes. Upon tribal council approval, they requested and received funding for operating their own reservation schools. The BIA and the Department of Education, both funding sources for these schools, were caught unaware of the pent-up desire for tribes to administer their own schools. As a dribble turned into what they perceived as an avalanche of new tribal schools, both these agencies began to question the wisdom of allowing so much autonomy to what they considered neophyte educators. They wanted to exercise some level of control, but they needed congressional approval to amend the Self-Determination Act. However, Congress was reluctant to approve any amendments without substantial evidence of the need to amend:

> In the Subcommittee Hearings, testimony provided on Indian education appropriations by the Assistant Secretary for Indian Affairs and the Director for the Office of Indian Education Programs (BIA) indicated that the BIA had published *Federal Rules and Regulations* for establishing educational standards for schools operated by the Department of Interior. The problem was that the standards would not apply to the Indian-controlled schools. Moreover, the Assistant Secretary expressed reservations about imposing standards on these schools in the light of current Indian Self-Determination Policies. As a result of this testimony and a Report of the Surveys and Investigations

Staff (House Appropriations), the House Subcommittee of the Department of the Interior and Related Agencies mandated that the Department of Education cooperate with the Bureau of Indian Affairs in performing an evaluation of Indian-controlled schools.[1]

Tribes refuted these allegations with evidence that they used the same nationally distributed standardized texts and tests and offered courses similar to those available in the public and BIA schools. They voiced a suspicion that the BIA and the Department of Education really wanted to undermine the spirit and intent of the Self-Determination Act.

Allegations went back and forth until finally the federal agencies testified that they were unable to meet the statutory requirements of the Self Determination Act, mandating certification that tribes provided educational services equal to or better than those previously administrated by the aforementioned agencies, because tribal schools had not followed state and federal educational codes.

The hearings led to a request for proposal (RFP) issued by the Department of Education in July 1984. ABT Associates received a contract to do the study. The (RFP) listed five objectives:

1. To provide a factual basis for evaluating specific concerns expressed by the Congress, relating to academic standards, costs and student attendance in Indian-controlled schools;

2. To document the Indian citizenship qualities, community values or cultural heritage which form a part of the educational objectives of these schools and to assist each of the schools participating in the study in developing appropriate methods for assessing their students with respect to such qualities;

3. To identify and provide tangible recognition for current graduates of participating schools who are judged to be outstanding with respect to uniform measures of academic achievement and locally administered evaluations of qualities identified in connection with the second objective;

4. To evaluate the role of Title IV Part A projects within the educational programs of participating schools; and

5. To document the response of affected members of the Indian community to this evaluation, and their views concerning it.[2]

"The first objective," stated the ABT in their final report, "directly related to the congressional mandate for an evaluation of Indian-controlled schools calls for three specific areas of inquiry. In the Department's Request for Proposals, these areas of inquiry were translated into the following expressly limited research questions:

1. *Academic Standards.* To what extent are graduates of Indian-controlled elementary and high schools equipped to do satisfactory work at the next higher level in publicly controlled schools?

2. *Costs.* Using data from BIA-operated and publicly controlled schools of comparable types and size, are staffing levels and payroll costs reasonable for the number of children actually served?

3. *Student Attendance.* To what extent is student attendance and persistence in school a serious problem?"[3]

Other important, but secondary objectives, ABT reported, were:

The study called for a documentation of the schools' educational objectives that reflect specifically Indian values or other qualities that cannot be assessed through standards tests of academic achievement. In addition, schools were to be assisted in developing alternative methods of assessing students with respect to these qualities.

The third objective is intended to provide recognition for the successes of Indian-controlled schools, as represented by their outstanding graduates.

The fourth objective relates to another concern of Congress, the high levels of funding for enrichment projects in Indian-controlled schools under Title IV Part A of the Educational Amendments of 1972 (The Indian Education Act). Specifically, the Request for Proposals sought an answer to the following research question:

Role of Title IV Projects. In what significant respects can it be demonstrated that activities supported by (the enrichment projects under Part A of the Indian Education Act) are genuinely *supplementary* to the basic education programs at schools which have been in operation more than three years?

The fifth objective of the evaluation—to document Indian community members' response to the evaluation and their views concerning it—recognizes that the design chosen for this evaluation might not be universally approved by those who would be affected by the study. Nonetheless, the study would have to rely on the voluntary cooperation of the Indian-controlled schools in whatever methods were undertaken. Therefore, this objective calls for documenting the extent of participation in the study by Indian-controlled schools and also requires the contractor to provide a forum for the expression of positive and negative views concerning the study.[4]

The Survey Pool

In October 1984, the Department of Education provided ABT Associates with a list of sixty-six Indian schools and organizations that received federal funding through the BIA and/or the Department of Education (Indian Education Title 4 part A).

Size, jurisdiction, or unwillingness to participate reduced the final data pool to twenty-two Indian-controlled schools. These Indian-controlled schools were matched with public and BIA schools in the same area which supposedly drew from the same reservation student pool. "The most important criterion for establishing a 'match,' said the report, was the degree of similarity between Indian students in the potential comparison school and in the Indian-controlled school."[5]

Measurements Used for Academic Achievement

Academic achievement was measured by the Comprehensive Tests of Basic Skills (CTBS), McGraw-Hill. The tests were administered by the teachers to students in grades eight and twelve in all of the schools participating in the survey. "The achievement comparisons for eighth graders were based on the nationally normed Normal Curve Equivalent (NCE) scores provided by the CTB/McGraw Hill Scoring Center. Nationally normed scores were not available for the High School and Beyond tests administered to twelfth graders. Therefore, the comparisons for these students were based on standardized scores for the study population."[6]

Findings on Student Achievement

The results of the ABT study for eighth and twelfth-grade students were as follows:

1. Achievement test scores for eighth graders in Indian-controlled schools are significantly lower than those for students in the comparison group.

2. No significant difference in test scores was found for twelfth graders in the sample, when compared with students in the comparison group.

3. Scores for BIA students in the twelfth grade sample act as a depressor on the mean for the comparison group. Scores for these students are significantly lower than the scores for students in Indian-controlled schools as well as public schools.[7]

School Attendance and Non-Academic Ratings

The study included attendance records and data collected of average daily membership, average daily attendance, aggregate days' absence, and number of students absent more than five days. They used two dates, October 1 and April 1, to collect the data.

Findings on School Attendance
and Pupil/Teacher Ratio

Average membership for Indian-controlled day schools was 191 compared to 494 for public schools. Indian-controlled schools evidence a ten to one pupil/teacher ratio, while public schools average seventeen pupils per teacher. When teacher aides and other direct instructional personnel (such as tutors) are factored into the calculation, the ratio for Indian-controlled schools becomes seven to one while the public-school ratio changes only slightly to sixteen students per teacher/aide.

Cost Analysis

The next objective, identifying school costs, compared Indian-controlled day schools and public schools and Indian-controlled boarding schools and BIA boarding schools. Three measurements were used to determine costs of operating the schools:

1. consolidated income and expense worksheets,

2. administrator questionnaires, and

3. instructional staff rosters

Findings on School Costs

The cost estimates are based on expense data for the 1983 through 1984 school year. Cost data on day schools and boarding schools were analyzed separately because of the substantial differences in expenditures (particularly for noninstructional salaries and food). Since all of the public schools are day schools and all of the BIA schools that provided cost data are boarding schools, this meant making two types of comparisons: Indian-controlled day schools vs. public schools and Indian-controlled boarding schools vs. BIA schools. However, they found the boarding-school sample was too small to be statistically measured with any accuracy. The major cost study found the following:

1. Total estimated average costs per pupil in Indian-controlled day schools are significantly higher than similarly estimated costs for the public schools in the comparison group for the 1983–84 fiscal year.

2. These estimated per pupil costs are higher for Indian-controlled schools in each of three major cost categories—instructional payroll, other payroll, and non-personnel costs.

3. When instructional payroll expenses are considered as a proportion of total expenses, the difference is marginally significant between Indian-controlled day schools and public schools. Differences in the proportion of non-personnel expense are highly significant.[8]

The report found significant differences in key factors related to school costs:

1. Indian-controlled day schools are significantly smaller (as expressed by average daily membership) than the public schools in the comparison group.

2. Pupil-teacher ratios for the Indian-controlled day schools are lower, i.e. there are fewer pupils per teacher in the Indian-controlled day schools than in public schools.

3. Teachers' salaries in Indian-controlled day schools are lower than teachers' salaries in our comparison group of public schools.[9]

The study found that in the Indian-controlled school, expenses per pupil totaled $6,890, compared to the public-school total of $3,505. Total payroll per pupil costs of Indian-controlled schools were $3,897, compared to $3,205 for public schools. Nonpersonnel costs in the Indian-controlled schools averaged $2,307, while public schools averaged $837.

The total average cost estimates per student for boarding-school students in ICS and BIA schools (1983–84) were $8,651 and $5,415 respectively. Instructional payroll per pupil in ICS schools totaled $2,435 in comparison to $1,732 for BIA schools. Non-personnel costs per pupil for ICS schools were $3,303 compared to $1,215 for BIA schools. The average membership of the ICS boarding schools was 285 compared to 644 for BIA boarding schools. Concerning the disparity between costs ABT reasoned, "The lower teacher-pupil ratio and the smaller class size in Indian-controlled schools, of course, reflect the fact that these schools have fewer students than do most public schools. However, these schools are required to offer similar course work and meet certain educational requirements (particularly at the secondary-school level). Thus they must employ teachers trained in specific areas."[10]

The report pointed out that there were substantial differences in nonpersonnel cost: "Indian-controlled boarding schools also evidence substantially higher nonpersonnel costs than do the BIA boarding schools. ICS per pupil costs for nonpersonnel expenses are close to three times higher than similar costs for BIA boarding schools."[11]

Title 4

Part A of the Indian Education Act (Title 4, PL 92-318), allocates[12] "grants to local education agencies (LEA's) to develop and operate elementary and secondary school programs specifically designed to meet the special educational and culturally related academic needs of Indian students."

Part A entitlement funds are driven by a weighted mathematical formula comprising the number of Indian children in a school, the average per pupil expenditure for the local school, and available appropriations. Under provisions of part A, any public, BIA, or Indian-controlled school with Indian student enrollment can apply for funds. The funds are relegated to programs that *supplement and not supplant* culturally related education experiences, but ABT focused exclusively on the ways Indian-controlled schools used these funds, and excluded data relating to the Bureau of Indian Affairs and public schools. This omission is interesting since these schools, particularly the public schools, have been the target of Indian complaints. ABT reasoned: "In the case of public schools, it would be easier to establish whether there had been maintenance of effort with respect to the education normally received by Indian and non-Indian students alike, and whether there had been special effort directed to the special educational and culturally related academic needs of Indian students."[13]

ABT justified the omission of comparative information because under part A there are several programs earmarked for Indian-controlled schools to establish and operate schools formerly operated by the BIA, and for enrichment programs, which in their view, differed from a section of part A designated for all local educational agencies' (LEA) (public, tribal, BIA) to meet the special educational or culturally academic needs of Indian children: "In Indian-controlled schools, where presumably the entire educational program has been designed with these special needs in mind, it is perhaps more difficult to distinguish between the basic educational activities that would characterize any school having similar resources, and supplemental activities designed specifically to meet the special educational needs of Indian students."[14]

Congress had earmarked both sections of part A separately, not for the purpose of differentiating between programmatic goals, but to assure that public and/or BIA schools should not have to compete with tribal schools who, under Indian preference, would have first priority and essentially lock out or minimize funding to public and BIA schools. The actual reason for not evaluating public and BIA Title 4 programs may never be known, but it is clear that Indian tribes use these funds to augment traditional Indian values and culture, while public and BIA schools normally focus on remedial reading or math classes. An argument can be made that both address programmatic goals, but it is clear that the former thinks in terms of multiculturalism and the later in terms of assimilation.

The evaluation found twenty-four ICS projects supported by Title 4, part A in fourteen schools. A perusal of the projects suggests a strong emphasis on traditional tribal values.[15] The objective or expected outcome of these projects ranged from improvement in basic academic skills, student retention, reduced dropout rate, better attendance, and reduced absenteeism, to improved student morale, reduced alcoholism and drug problems, improved health conditions, improved job/life skills, increased respect for elders, and increased community involvement (see table 3.1).

Findings on Title 4

The ABT report states:

We conclude that for schools participating in this evaluation the activities and services funded by Title IV Part A enrichment projects are indeed "supplementary" to the basic education

Table 3.1   Learning Priorities of Indian-Controlled Schools

Projects	Number
Enrichment classes: art and art careers, animal husbandry, environmental science, computer science, career ed, etc.	6
Direct instruction in traditional arts and crafts, music, language, history, etc.	5
Culturally-relevant curriculum or learning-resource development for math, science, social studies, English	4
Traditional curriculum or learning-resource development for traditional arts and crafts, music, language, history, etc.	2
Basic skills enrichment/individualized remedial instruction	2
Student services: home-school coordinator, advisors, dorm counselors, activities director	2
Chemical abuse/health education	1
Recreation program, emphasizing rewards for attendance and good behavior	1
Establishment of library facilities and services	1

program. For the most part, the activities and services funded by the Part A projects provide enrichment experiences of variations in instructional content and approach that otherwise would not be available to the students in these schools. In addition, these activities and services are designed to alleviate special educational and/or culturally related academic problems that are prevalent among low-income, minority students—i.e. low achievement, high drop-out rates and high absenteeism.[16]

It is not surprising that the tribal projects are certified as supplementary, because in fact the scope and breadth of these courses are at the heart of the reasons why tribal schools exist. Traditional tribal instruction was and is not available for students attending the BIA and/or public schools: "We were not asked to determine the cost effectiveness of these strategies, and we have no data that would support such an analysis. Some of the projects have relatively high per-pupil costs, while others are very modest in cost. Whether the expense is worthwhile would have to be determined through rigorous evaluation of the individual projects."[17]

Here's where "different scales for different whales" comes into play. It is unlikely that ABT or any other organization could have assessed efficacy using the melting-pot philosophy because the intent of these projects was to develop multiculturalism, a way by which Indian students matured strongly centered in their own culture while surrounded by non-Indian culture. In any case, the federal requirements call for annual reports of the projects, not for a cost-benefit analysis substantiating the projects.

Criteria for Nonacademic Ratings

One aspect of the study was to include high-achievement awards for students. Part of the criteria was based upon academic excellence and part upon the school's own nonacademic rating system. In the interest of brevity, the top four criteria of each school follow.

Oneida

1. Oneida language
2. Oneida culture

3. Oneida Law

4. Self-concept/attitude.

Borrego Pass

1. Ability to speak and understand good conversational Navajo.

2. Ability to read and write Navajo.

3. Ability to interpret concepts and ideas from English to Navajo and from Navajo to English.

4. Public-speaking ability in both Navajo and English.

Ojibwa

1. Carry responsibility well; can be counted on to do what he/she has promised and usually do it well.

2. Self-confident with children his/her own age as well as adults; seem comfortable when asked to show his/her work to the class.

3. Seem to be well liked by his/her classmates.

4. Cooperative with teacher and classmates; tend to avoid bickering and generally easy to get along with.

Kickapoo Nation

1. Citizenship

2. Leadership

3. Behavior

4. Motivation.

St. Stephens

1. School citizenship

2. Character

3. Community involvement.

4. Traditional involvement.

Paschal Sherman

1. Behavior/attitudes: classroom, playground, and lunchroom behavior; attitude during school day.

2. Athletics: participation in varsity sports;

3. Improvement in attendance over grade 7.

4. Four Winds Indian Club participation, crafts, attendance, fundraising, leadership.

Marty

1. Awareness of ethnic values and traditions; self-awareness as an Indian youth

2. Self-image: self-worth and self-awareness

3. Courtesy: respect for others

4. Attendance and punctuality: accountability and dependability.

These criteria are further evidence of the importance tribal schools place on the acquisition of tribal values, including fluent use of language and the norms of tribal society.

Community Response

ABT conducted a series of regional meetings early in the contract to review the study design with groups of Indian-controlled school administrators. The "community response" measurement analyzed unstructured interviews of regional meetings. ABT also sent out monthly evaluation bulletins and distributed them among ICS administrators and other interested parties on a mailing list provided by the Department of Education. This bulletin provided current information on the progress of the study, identified critical next steps requiring the schools' active cooperation or participation, and summarized important design decisions. The bulletin provided information on a toll-free telephone number for calls to American Indian Technical Services' Denver office. A third method was a set of open-ended interview questions that were asked at the time of the field visits to Indian-controlled schools.

ABT distributed draft copies of the final report to all currently funded Indian-controlled schools, including those not participating in the evaluation and to other interested parties identified by the Department of Education. The report said:

> In commissioning this evaluation, the Department of Education recognized that, of many possible designs, only one could be chosen, and that one design might not be universally approved by members of the Indian communities who would be affected. The Department therefore included in the study contract an explicit requirement to document "the response of affected members of the Indian community to this evaluation and their views concerning it."[18]

The community evaluation requirement in the regulations governing the research project was included in order to gain the voluntary cooperation of the Indian-controlled schools and to provide a forum for dissenting voices to be heard.

The regional meetings were held in Aberdeen (SD), Albuquerque (NM), Minneapolis (MN), and Spokane (WA) during the week of December 4 through 8, 1984. Twenty-eight schools were represented at the meetings, which were attended by up to twenty people from each region. "With few exceptions," the report said, "the ICS representatives voiced an intent to cooperate with the evaluation." At the same time, they voiced serious objections regarding the evaluation methods (especially those for assessing costs and achievement). Some of their concerns follow:

1. Is it fair or relevant to compare Indian-controlled schools with BIA or public schools that are quite different from them in goals and objectives, resources and constraints, and the length of time they have been in operation? Why not assess the Indian-controlled schools in terms of their own growth since becoming contract schools or in comparison to the schools that they replaced (e.g., on achievement)?

2. Since contract schools often serve a very different kind of Indian student from those in nearby public schools, how can the evaluation team be sure of an adequate match between student groups for the comparison of achievement and absenteeism? (Administrators believed Indian students in the contract schools were more often from lower income, more traditional, less acculturated families.)

3. Is it fair to compare academic achievement only at the eighth and twelfth grade levels, since (a) most of the older students have received only a small proportion of their education in Indian-controlled schools; and (b) according to some administrators, Indian students are likely to persist through the twelfth grade in public schools only if they are high achievers and dropout if they are low achievers.

4. What is the purpose of the detailed cost study? How can the evaluation team be fair in comparing costs. Will they, for instance, include all the resources available to public schools in their analysis? Why is it necessary to examine detailed expenditures if this is not a study of fiscal accountability?[19]

The ICS representatives requested revisions in the scope and design of the ABT study. They wanted the study to document the historical context of Indian-controlled schools and compare them to the quality of education previously provided to Indian children (in many cases, in the same schools formerly run by the BIA, now tribally operated). They requested that comparisons take into account the goals and objectives of each of these types of schools, the resources and constraints and characteristics of the Indian students served, and reexamine the purpose and scope of the data collection with reference to the cost study:

Each of these suggestions had some merit, and we seriously considered whether to include them in the study design. However, based in part on direction from the Department of Education, we determined that most of the suggestions were not feasible and that the resources and aims of the study were narrower than many of the suggestions imply. We did, however, reduce the scope of the cost study, moving away from a detailed examination of both personnel and non-personnel costs by type of activity.[20]

Time Allocated for Field Research

The research team made site visits to twenty-eight Indian-controlled schools and twenty-seven comparison schools between April 22 and May 17, 1985. On the average, the ABT team spent one and a half calendar days per visit to an Indian-controlled school and one calendar day per visit to a comparison school. In that time it collected the data required for the evaluation.

Intervening Factors

The report admits that matching the three types of schools was virtually impossible. One of the problems the team faced was that the majority of Indian-controlled schools are either primary or secondary, while the public schools have primary, middle, and high-school levels. Another problem was the size of the student body. Two-thirds of the Indian-controlled schools enrolled fewer than two-hundred pupils compared with one-third of the public schools and one out of six BIA schools. The average enrollment for the Indian-controlled school in the sample was 201; for public schools, 351; and for BIA schools, 512.[21]

Another factor influencing the outcome of the study was that five of the six BIA schools were boarding schools and only five of the twenty-eight Indian-controlled schools had boarding students.

Finally, both the BIA and the public schools were part of a larger system that helped to reduce costs, while the Indian-controlled schools were stand-alone schools, responsible for the entire cost of every piece of equipment, thus making overhead expenses far higher than those of the BIA and/or public schools.

Comparison of Student Backgrounds

In spring 1985, a questionnaire was administered to eighth-
and twelfth-grade students in the study group. It was found that
students in both the eighth and the twelfth grades were at about
the same age level and were evenly divided by sex. But while roughly
75 percent of the students enrolled in the Indian-controlled school
had parents who were tribally enrolled, only 50 percent of the
eighth-grade students and 60 percent of the twelfth-grade students
in the public schools had parents on the tribal rolls. In the BIA
schools, the proportion of students with both parents on tribal rolls
was less than 50 percent for eighth graders and about 75 percent
for twelfth graders.

To determine the socioeconomic status (SES), of the students'
families, ABT used the following indicators: father and mother's
education, employment, and family income and whether they
received a daily newspaper, had an encyclopedia or other reference
books in the home, a typewriter, an electric dishwasher, two or more
working vehicles, more than fifty books, a room of their own, a
pocket calculator, a color TV, or a telephone.

"The ICS students appear to be from families with much lower
incomes on average than students in public schools. The average
income for ICS students is around $9,000 per year, while the average
for public school students is around $13,000. (The mean for BIA
students is about $10,000)."[22]

Language or bilingualism was also surveyed. ABT asked three
questions: "What was the first language you spoke when you were
a child?" "What language do you usually speak now?" "What language do the people in your home usually speak?" Sixty-six percent
of the twelfth-grade students in public schools have the lowest possible score on bilingualism, compared with 45 percent of the students
in Indian-controlled schools and only 9 percent of the students in
BIA schools. Thirty-five percent of the twelfth graders in BIA schools
have the highest possible score on bilingualism.[23]

Educational Aspirations

When twelfth graders were asked, "Do you plan to go to college
at some time in the future" 74 percent of ICS seniors and 68 percent
of both BIA and public-school seniors said they expected to attend
college at some time in the future.

Location of Residence

Students were asked to describe where they live while attending school, as an indicator of their geographic isolation. The most vivid finding is that, across all three groups, the majority of students are from extremely small, rural communities. The study found that 77 percent of ICS students live in the smallest communities, compared with 67 percent of students in public schools.

Years in Current School and Percent of Education under Similar Auspices

The study found that twelfth-grade students were the least likely to have attended the same school for at least two years. Of the ICS students, 79 percent had attended the same school at least two years, compared with 97 percent of the BIA and public schools.

The differences were expected. Approximately half the Indian-controlled schools in the sample were established since 1975, and one quarter were established since 1978. Therefore, in many of the communities studied, there were no alternatives to BIA or public schools, when these students started their education. Moreover, in many communities, the Indian-controlled schools have developed a reputation for successfully educating students who have had learning or adjustment problems in public schools, or who may be in danger of dropping out. Some make special efforts to reach out to students who have left school or who are referred by the courts or penal system. For these students, the Indian-controlled school serves as an "alternative school" or "continuation school," which they may attend after many years in the public school system.

The study found no significant differences between the groups on age, sex, standard of living, or educational aspirations for eighth or twelfth graders. The variables that were significantly different for both grade levels include parents' tribal enrollment, mother's education, miles traveled to school, years in current school, and percent of education under similar auspices.[24]

It is worth noting that in most cases, it is not the ICS groups that had the unusual distribution. That is, on most variables, if the ICS students are different from students in one type of school in the control group, they are also similar to students in the other type of control; or, alternatively, they fall somewhere between the two groups. (It should be noted that the two control groups are not equal in size, however.) The exceptions to this are, for eighth graders, parents' tribal enrollment—higher percentages of ICS students have parents who are enrolled tribal members than either BIA or public school students; and location of residence—the ICS students on the average, live in smaller communities. For twelfth graders, ICS students are much less likely than BIA or public school students to have attended the same school at least two years. Finally, for both grade levels, ICS students have spent much less time in school under similar auspices than have either the BIA or public school student.[25]

Conclusion

The Department of Education ordered an evaluation of tribal schools for political objectives, and the guidelines they issued in their RFP reflect that intent. They disapproved of tribal schools adopting tribal educational codes independent of state or federal regulations and requested congressional amendments to force tribes to adopt state or federal regulations.[26] They were obliged, under the statutory regulations of the Self-Determination Act to evaluate programs receiving funds from the Department of Education and maintained they could not fulfill their obligations under the existing rules of the act. Congress would not act without evidence that tribal regulations weakened or constricted educational standards in tribal schools. The solution proposed by the Department of Education was a comparison between tribal, public, and BIA schools assessing and comparing academic achievement of Indian students in selected schools.[27] Had they really been interested in assessing tribal school efficacy, they would have first issued an RFP to design effective measurements reflecting tribal-school multiculturalim, rather than the melting-pot context and then issued an RFP to conduct a study under those guidelines. At the very least, they could have provided flexibility for ABT to include the issues raised by the Indian community at the ABT regional meetings.

ABT is a well-known, highly credible educational-assessment corporation, and yet ABT carried out the evaluation even though it knew the tribal schools selected and Indian students attending these schools were not a comparative "match." To its credit ABT did not cover up the mis-match, but it is too savvy not to have known from the onset it was comparing apples with oranges. This was a political not an educational decision.

The heavy hand of political control is endemic throughout this evaluation, but the worst part is the attack on multiculturalism under the guise of "quality" education.[28] Multiculturalism is a fact of life, but it has gained little more than lip service from local or national educational bureaucracy. Tribal schools do not shrink from the genocidal history that is glossed over in public and BIA schools. Nor do they minimize the contributions of Indians to the well-being of present day America. They teach that 48 percent of the world's agricultural crops were developed by the Indians of the Americas; the pharmaceutical world originated through the knowledge of Indian medicine men and women; the adobe buildings that dot the southwestern landscape originated with the architecture of the pueblos; the kayak, the parka, and sunglasses, are Eskimo inventions; the Quonset hut is an Iroquois design, and even the concept of a strong central government and sovereign states comes from the Iroquois. The history of America did not begin with Columbus, but instead began with a vast and complex civilization existing thousands of years before the arrival of Europeans on this continent.

Cultural pluralism is one of those notions that people say they value but seldom practice. We are the only nation in the world that thinks it is un-American for a child to speak more than one language in the home. There was a bill before Congress in 1989 to make English the official language of the United States. This is a nation of American Indians and immigrants, and no one language should dominate national policy any more than any one religion: "Although the overall extent of cultural bias in the schools is difficult to measure, there are a number of indicators that underlie the seriousness of the problem. Studies conducted in urban high schools have revealed dropout rates as high as 85 percent for Native Americans."[29]

Tribal schools offer Indian children comfort in being who they are and a safe haven to learn about themselves and the world around them. They are multicultural precisely because Indian Country wants Indian children to function in both societies. They have not had the time to mature as other school systems have, but even so they have become a political threat to the entrenched educational establishment.

4

Analysis of ABT Research

Persistent budget cuts in education at every level of government have been disastrous for the American education system. Indian children are even more shortchanged by budget cuts because they are most vulnerable to the shortsightedness of policy framers. Programs designed to address multicultural pluralism are the first to be axed. Innovative programs, the purchase of more sophisticated textbooks, and teacher education classes that address multicultural pluralism all fall by the wayside when local systems face state and federal cuts.

As these federal subsidies dwindle, so does advocacy of multicultural education by local school boards. School boards are merely reacting to the lack of public support for special programs, once made tolerable only by the federal dollars brought into local school systems. Local newspapers are quick to pick up on long-standing arguments of persistent drop-out rates among minorities and disparage the profound historical and contemporary impact of institutional racism.

If you ask average Americans what they know about Indians, they will rattle off the words *corn, Thanksgiving day* and *Christopher Columbus* followed by *alcoholism, tomahawk,* and *scalping.* The myths persist, and they play a large role in the way communities and their representatives on school boards dismiss Indian student failure as an aberration, rather than a systemic failure. It is asking a lot of Indian children psychologically to handle all the negative stereotypes they confront in the classroom and at the same time, envision him as doctors, lawyers, engineers, teachers, and scientists.

51

The logical place to begin any inquiry into Indian education is the classroom. What texts are being used, and how are they being used? How do Indian children respond to Indian teachers, and how are different teaching modalities affecting student achievement? How involved are Indian parents or local Indian communities in the school systems? ABT did not examine the classroom, the textbooks, teaching styles, learning environments or communities, and it did not talk to parents.

The ABT study relied heavily on statistical data to substantiate educational achievement, but a serious and critical analysis should have gone beyond that elemental level.[1] The ABT goal of evaluating the efficacy of Indian-controlled schools was weakened by the methodology of the study. The study professed to match Indian students in all three types of schools. The evidence it presented for this "match" was that schools in the same area, drew from the same Indian student population. But the student populations were completely different, invalidating their claim for a matched or controlled study.

Student Populations

There is a marked difference between students attending tribal schools and those attending the BIA and public schools. Tribal school students typically have traditional family backgrounds, family income of about $9,000 a year, and tribally enrolled parents who speak Indian as a primary language. However, ABT found that 60 percent of the Indian student population who attend public school have only one tribally enrolled parent, speak English as a primary language, and have a family income of $13,000 a year. Students attending BIA schools had fewer ties with their tribe, tribal language, and traditions, although family income is about the same ($10,000).

In fact, there is a continuum. The stronger the tie Indian children have to tribal language, tradition, and culture, the more likely they will attend tribal school, if available. When attendance in a tribal school is not an option, these same children will likely attend BIA schools, preferring them to public schools because some classmates come from the same tribe or region. Only when neither of these options is available will Indian students from traditional backgrounds attend public schools. They will be a minority even among Indian students, because the majority of public-school Indian students use English as a primary language and have fewer ties to their culture. With this in mind, the ABT "match" has only one common denominator. These children are Indian.

Once the language, income, and cultural inconsistencies were known, ABT should have stopped and examined the research methodology for a more valid study. For instance, they could have taken a cue from the Indian community and compared the academic performance of ICS students with those attending the same school under former BIA management. It is likely that prior to admission, many ICS and BIA students attended public schools. The study would have had great value to educators if they had gone back to the public-school records and examined Indian student academic levels in public schools prior to attending Indian schools. In addition, it is bewildering that the ABT study did not evaluate the use of Title 4 funding in the public or BIA schools. Presumably, the schools received federal Title 4 funds to improve educational attainment of Indian students, but we are left in the dark concerning the amount school districts received, the projects they designed, the proposed outcome, and the success or failure of these projects.

Student Achievement

The crux of the ABT study was to ascertain whether ICS students were on par with Indian students attending public and BIA schools. The report found no appreciable difference between the three types of schools in Indian student achievement in the twelfth grade. The findings must have disappointed the Department of Education and the Bureau of Indian Affairs, because they had hoped the difference would be dramatic evidence of a need to amend the Self-Determination Act permitting these agencies to regulate ICS schools. Even more dramatic was the SES evidence that ICS students came from poorer families (mean income of $9,000 compared to public-school Indian student families of $13,000 and BIA student families of $10,000). ICS students scored higher on the achievement tests than the BIA students. This fact is a humbling reminder to educators everywhere. In the long run, it is not the poverty of students or the experience of school systems that determines the academic success of students. It is high aspirations.

Indian-controlled schools succeed because they function within the culture, norms, and traditions of Indian communities and subsequently engage parents as formidable allies in the educational mission. Comfortable children integrate the aspirations of school and home. It does not matter whether the students are Amish,

Jewish, black, or Indian. When schools reflect the aspirations of the community, when classrooms are congruent with their world, children learn.[2]

It is possible, in fact probable, that the evidence would have been even more dramatic had the study included state and national norms. There is no evidence that ICS students would have achieved equity with state or national norms, but neither would the students from BIA or public schools, two systems with a century of experience. Also, since the state and national norms are a yardstick for determining readiness for higher education, it might have been helpful to determine whether the higher education aspirations of Indian students (74 percent of ICS seniors and 68 percent of BIA and public school seniors) was realistic.

School Costs

The cost of educating three distinctly different populations and school settings varied widely. Public schools have had a long time to purchase audio-visual materials, textbooks, and computers, and they can spread out these purchases over a period of time, because they generally know in advance what budget they have to work with. BIA schools have also been able to purchase equipment over a long period of time. ICS schools are funded year to year and must make purchases over a short period of time, since they are new to the education system. It is not surprising the study found that "total estimated average costs per pupil in Indian controlled day schools are significantly higher than similarly estimated costs for the public schools in our comparison group for the 1983–84 fiscal year."

The cost of public-school education varies from area to area. Many public schools have reduced their costs by including Indian entitlement money into the general fund. School districts can make bulk purchases and enjoy considerable discounts from vendors. Left out of this discussion is how comparable the costs of public schools in this study are to state, regional, or national costs of public education: "When instructional payroll expenses are considered as a proportion of total expenses, the difference is marginally significant between Indian controlled day schools and public schools. Differences in the proportion of non-personnel expense are highly significant."

Nonpersonnel expenses include food, books, field trips requiring rental or purchase of vehicles, maps, slides, projectors, video cassettes, and films. They also include the hiring of curriculum development experts to develop bilingual teaching materials. ICS considers these expenditures a priority, while public and BIA schools view them as nonessential. Nonpersonal costs also include travel expenditures of parent committees to attend meetings. Public and BIA schools consider these activities peripheral to education. Indian-controlled schools treat these expenditures as integral to their education mission. These philosophical differences account for the seemingly large difference between the $2,307 spent by Indian-controlled schools and the $837 spent by public schools. The study also found significant differences in key factors related to school costs, that is,

1. Indian controlled day schools are significantly smaller (as expressed by average daily membership) than the public schools in our comparison group.

2. Pupil-teacher ratios for the Indian controlled day schools are lower, i.e. there are fewer pupils per teacher in the Indian controlled day schools than in public schools.

3. Teachers' salaries in Indian controlled day schools are lower than teachers' salaries in our comparison group of public schools.

Indian-controlled schools are small and more expensive in the short run. In the long run, substantial savings can be realized as potential dropouts graduate. There appears to be growing evidence that the past trend of consolidating schools as a cost benefit may correlate negatively with increased drop-out rates. Lower national test scores suggest that larger schools increase the likelihood of at-risk students getting lost in a system.[3] ICS schools will always be small, because the Indian population is only 1 percent of the national population. The question is not whether they are small, ergo more expensive, but whether Indian children are receiving effective education which will enable them to lead productive adult lives.

Political Implications of the ABT Study

The impetus for the ABT study was federal uneasiness about ICS education standards. But there was a hidden political agenda. As one commissioner of Indian affairs put it, "Our Indian Schools should be building better Americans, not better Indians." This philosophy conflicts with that of the Indian Education Assistance and

Self-Determination Act committing the federal government to support, financially as well as philosophically, the concept of Indian
'self-rule.'

There is no question that Indian tribal schools should be monitored, but with an even hand. Indian education funds are used by
public and Bureau of Indian Affairs schools, and if evaluations have
any meaning, all schools and programs using these funds should
be monitored using the same yardstick. How else can effectiveness
be measured? The "standards" heretofore mentioned during the
congressional hearings, address the number of courses and course
subjects, not academic achievement. To this day, federal Indian
education dollars go to schools that fail to educate Indian children.
Tribal schools exist precisely because other school systems have
failed to educate Indian children.

The myth that segregated tribal schools handicap Indian children for a comfortable adult transition into the larger society over-
looks the reality that many young people attend private and
parochial schools without apparent trauma, as well as the wealth
of information children receive in this electronic age. Tribal schools
do not separate, but rather integrate, the Indian child with both
nations, the tribe and the United States. These schools operate on the
premise that Indian children are capable of entering professional
careers while remaining culturally and emotionally Indian.

Public and BIA education reflect the philosophy that Indian
children must assimilate in order to function outside of the reservation. They take the position that entry into medical school entails
assimilation, and by that we mean complete absorption of the values, norms, and roles of the larger society. This leaves children
growing up without a center. A fragmented child matures into a
dependent, fearful, angry adult, and society loses one more Indian
to alcoholism, crime, and despair. The price Indian children pay
when systems deny them access and integration to their tribal roots
is staggering.

Tribal schools provide concrete role models that Indian values
and traditions are not incongruent with a future as a teacher, principal, doctor, lawyer, or tribal leader. Freed from societal stereotyping,
Indian children grow into critical thinkers, capable of taking charge
of their lives. Critical thinking generates self-worth, a vision of one's
place in society, responsibility (as Indians) to a tribe, a region, a
country.

The bona fide measurement of education is how highly a student has developed critical thinking. A test that can assess that skill
also tells us something about the quality of education. Any teacher

in any classroom can convey facts. If a teacher repeats a statement two or three times, students will automatically put that statement into notes or underline the statement in a textbook. Testing that statement is not testing the quality of education. Take, for example, a particularly odious statement taught to every school-age child: Christopher Columbus discovered America. Say it three or four times in class, combined with the date, and students will automatically store the information. Enter researchers. Use that as a test question. Scores rise. Critical thinking is not being tested.

Suppose the same fact was given in a tribal school. There would be some discussion about Columbus. Was it discovery or invasion? Whom did he meet when he landed at San Salvador? What were the Arawaks like? When Spanish writers described them, were they describing the tribe or their perceptions of this tribe? How did they communicate? What led Columbus to sail across the ocean? Was personal ambition one of his characteristics, or was it curiosity? Is personal ambition an evil thing in itself? When and under what conditions are people's personal ambitions and society's needs mediated? What role did religion play in Columbus's society, and what role did it play in the Arawaks' development of culture? What happened to the tribe that met Columbus? Why? What were the societal assumptions of European cultures and of American Indian cultures? Are they different today?

These are only some of the questions that could be raised to develop critical thinking. They are more likely to be raised in Indian-controlled schools because they use nationally distributed textbooks. These texts are value-laden. Indian culture and history contradict much of the materials students must read and learn. The challenge of tribal schools is to use these texts in ways that develop critical thinking. This is not what is measured by standard testing. The problem with relying for information on a single day's visit to a school as ABT did is that one must rely upon testing data, which in itself does not address critical thinking, or for that matter, the quality of education.

"We are a nation at risk," wrote former Secretary of Education Terrel H. Bell: "We report to the American people that while we can take justifiable pride in what our schools and colleges have historically accomplished and contributed to the United States and the well-being of its people, the educational foundations of our society are presently *being eroded by a rising tide of mediocrity* that threatens our very future as a Nation and a people."[4]

The "rising tide of mediocrity" is the direct consequence of institutional racism inherent in the public and BIA schools. These schools demand that an Indian child choose between the past and the future. And when confused Indian children respond by failing, the system assumes the failure was the fault of the Indian student. Tribal schools are a remedy, experimental and untested, but lacking a complete overhaul of the public and BIA systems, the best solution to a thorny problem.

5

The Madison Study: The Town, the Reservation, the Ethos

The Town

Madison is a small, sleepy town in a rural western state, three miles from an Indian reservation. There are probably no more than five hundred people who live, do business, and/or work in Madison or the large ranches and farms circling the town.

The main street of the town has a Safeway, a movie house (open only on weekends), a sandwich and/or breakfast diner, a western clothing store, a restaurant that serves dinner, a five and ten shop and a movie-rental store. A convenience store off the main street stays open until ten o'clock in the evening, and there are a few tourist stores that sell local crafts and used furniture. The movie-rental store is the only business owned and operated by Indians. Once the sun goes down, all human activity flows indoors.

The local bank is a branch of a state-wide bank. The tribe uses this branch for all of its financial transactions, including project funds. Except for the maintenance crew, only whites are employed in the bank. Other commercial enterprises, such as local construction companies and electrical and farm supply stores rarely hire Indians except for menial short-term jobs. Jobs are scarce for everyone in Madison, but especially for the Indians.

Madison has a local newspaper. There is no serious attempt to cover news about reservation activities. Tribal council members have testified before the U.S. Congress, been appointed by the White

House to significant positions in government, and received degrees from Harvard, but the news is buried on the back page, if it is mentioned at all.

Main Street has a couple of bars with pool tables in the back. They function primarily as community meeting and recreation centers. Indian, and non-Indian drink quite a lot in Madison, and no one is surprised to see anyone drunk. The perception of the townspeople though, is that Indians are the primary drunks.

It behooves a Madison resident to stay healthy, because medical care is scarce, and the nearest hospital is about thirty miles away in the next town. The town has a grammar school and a high school. The visibly deteriorated high school is sectioned off into a middle school and a high school. Madison has not supported capital outlay school funds for ten years. The townspeople have made the decision to hold off repairing, renovating, or remodeling the schools because the mayor of the town, who also is senior faculty member of the high school, knows that sooner or later the federal government will fund building a new high school because of increased Indian student enrollment.[1]

People who live in the center of town are poor or of marginal income, eking out a bare-bones living operating small service businesses, such as the hairdresser who runs her operation from her home. The town is too small to support a McDonald's or Wendy's. Existing businesses service large farms and ranches.

Major purchases, such as clothes or appliances, are available in a town that is about thirty miles away. Those who can afford it make major purchases in a city which is about an hour's drive from Madison where there is a greater selection of merchandise. These shopping patterns by Madison residents prevent the development of an economic infrastructure in the town. The middle-class income earned by tribal and school personnel constitute substantial economic buying power, but Madison is too small to support a shopping center or department store. Consequently, discretionary money is spent outside of the town, limiting the ability of Madison to grow or employ its citizens.

Except for new school teachers, few people move to Madison. Most current residents were born and educated in Madison. In the morning, you can find ranch hands and ranch owners having breakfast side-by-side in the local diner. They have known one another since childhood and greet each other with unrestrained enthusiasm every morning. Indians and non-Indians feel free to talk to one another, sometimes over several tables, about the price of wheat or beef, the impending drought, and commodities on the stock exchange. These bread and butter issues are peppered with gossip about the local high-school football team (in the winter), baseball team (in the summer), and what was on television the night before.

While democracy is evident in the diner and other commercial establishments, a caste system is evident as well. At the diner, Indians sit in a corner, away from the mainstream traffic. This is an age-old habit. Everyone expects it, and no one thinks much about it. No one is impolite, but if two couples come into the diner or restaurant at the same time, or even if an Indian couple comes in first, the white couple is served first. It is the way things are done. The same automatic response can be observed walking down the narrow sidewalks of Main Street. When Indians and non-Indians walking in opposite directions approach one another, the Indians move toward the curb and the whites toward the store windows. It is expected.

Owner-occupied houses that dot the landscape of Madison are well-kept brick, generally two story, with spacious porches, neat manicured lawns, and flower beds. There are no swimming pools in this area, perhaps because of the scarcity of water, and perhaps because of the cost. Besides, summer season is short.

Since the vast majority of residents in Madison own their own homes, a renter is clearly on the low echelon of the social milieu. Rental homes are built one on top of another (this in an area where land is inexpensive) and appear run-down, with peeling paint, broken windows, and absence of lawns or flower beds. Rent is high considering the depressed economy of the area. Some families will spend half of their income putting a roof over their heads. Most renters are Indians who cannot get into the housing project on the reservation or those who simply cannot afford a home.

Cable TV is available, and some residents own satellite dishes. Cable is the major source of national and international news in this rural area. Only an outsider can feel the isolation of this town from the rest of the country or even the rest of the state. Residents do not perceive this, or if they do, they welcome it as an oasis from the rest of the world. For them, living in Madison may be economically precarious, but it is safe, predictable, and protected from the evils of the city and from the problems of the rest of the world.

Few travel, except to a spectacular federal National Park famous the world over. Vacations are taken locally either to this site, in Canada, or to neighboring rural states. Camping out is a favorite vacation lifestyle, and many have travel trailers. Those who venture to San Francisco or Disneyland return with the old cliché "nice place to visit, but I wouldn't want to live there."

Madison's professional class includes some doctors and lawyers, teachers and administrators, and a sprinkling of college-trained personnel working for the newspaper or in the farming/ranching sector, but most people consider themselves educated if they graduate from high school.

The power elite in Madison consists of the mayor (also a school teacher), bank president, newspaper editor, wealthy ranchers, and in a secondary but pivotal role, members of the school board and school administration. Teachers play a major role as power brokers. Nothing ever gets done without some consensus by the power elite, including building, zoning, and hiring and firing from any significant economic position.

College tuition in this state is very inexpensive, but the nearest college is about an hour away, and the major state university is about eight hours' drive from Madison. This makes college education more expensive than that of neighboring western states, since attending college usually means either long drives to and from campus or moving onto campus.

The out migration of young, educated people from Madison increases with each year, but most of the citizens of Madison were born, raised, educated to the high-school level, live and work within a thirty-mile radius of the town. In spite of the out-migration pattern of the college educated, most of the power elite consider high-school preparation for college entry as important to the next generation.

There is a strong conservative streak at every income level in this community. On one hand, the power elite loathe government restrictions or regulatory ordinances, perceiving these as violations of individual rights. Government, they feel, especially the federal government, should be at arm's length. On the other hand, the power elite was willing for a generation of young people to be schooled in inadequate facilities so that they would qualify for federal subsidies.

This sleepy little town of Madison was the center of one of the most heated and passionately fought controversies in education. Eventually the conflict enveloped the town's school board, the State Board of Education, the U.S. Department of Education, the U.S. Civil Rights Commission, and ultimately Indian academicians from California who were hired to evaluate and assess the extent of the complaints lodged by the reservation three miles away.

The Reservation

The Indian reservation is about three miles away from Madison, separated from the town by a river. This river became famous when it was the focus of federal litigation at the turn of the century. Ranchers who had homesteaded land north of the reservation (that was once reservation land) dammed the river to guarantee water for their cattle and crops. This left little water downstream for the Indians. To guarantee water to the reservation, the federal government sued the ranchers on behalf of the tribe. The suit was successful and became the centerpiece of national Indian water rights. This and other suits confirmed suspicions of Madison's white residents that Indians were getting a "free ride" by the federal government and have stiffened an already strong conservative streak among Madison's townspeople.

Tribal membership numbers about 4,200, but approximately 2,800 live on or near the reservation. The 675,147-acre reservation is divided like a triangle, two points bordering two very small non-Indian towns, the third point leading to the heart of more traditional reservation Indians. These traditionals maintain minimal contact with the non-Indians of Madison.

The traditional Indian community has a tribal school. The area of the community is about twenty-eight miles. The entire reservation is so extremely rural, one can drive south to north of the two points measuring forty miles from Madison to Centerville without seeing another person, except for an occasional hitchhiker.

The brick tribal office is large and sprawling, built during the seventies as part of the War on Poverty projects. Adjacent to the tribal office is a building that houses the Indian community college an Indian owned and operated grocery store, and a restaurant. To one side of the tribal office is a gymnasium and an indoor swimming pool, a source of recreation both for the Indians and for the non-Indians who want to swim or play basketball. The recreation facilities are open to all residents of the reservation and the town of Madison. Adjacent to the gym is a senior citizens' center. Indians are living longer these days, and they use the center to meet, eat, and enjoy myriad activities. The center is the least controversial and most popular program on the reservation. On the other side of the tribal office is the public health center and emergency hospital. Nearby is an alcoholic rehabilitation center that detoxes and houses recovering alcoholics. There is also a small house that stores surplus books, donated by publishing companies. The collection consists of such diverse selections as Gray's Anatomy and a biography of Marilyn Monroe, each priced at twenty-five cents. Also available are new tapes and the history of Gaul during Caesar's time. The twenty-five-cent fee covers shipping expenses.

Nearby is a huge, empty brick building, a relic from the era of Bureau of Indian Affairs operations on the reservations. One of the concerns of the tribe is to put this building into use for some sort of economic or job-training function. It would also make an excellent facility for hydroponic farming. The growing season is very short in this area. Hydroponic farming may be a solution to the high price of fruit and vegetables that come from California and other warm-weather states.

Most of the programs formerly run by the BIA are now under tribal contract. The tribe is governed by a twelve-man council. There is no reason women cannot be on the council, but very few women ever run for office, and even fewer have been elected. Besides the guaranteed paycheck (rare on a reservation where programs are funded year by year), being a member of a tribal council has numerous rewards, much the same as being mayor of a city or governor of a state. There's the obvious perk for any politician: being able to mete out rewards to friends and sanctions to enemies.

The not-so-obvious perk that is prized by council members is the extensive travel necessary to negotiate contracts or partake in federal contract-training programs. Training sessions are important educational tools on this as on any reservation. There are some members of the council who attended or graduated from college, but of the twelve, the majority have only completed high school. This is not usually seen as a benefit or as a liability. Council members are elected because of personal attributes as opposed to specific training. A degree in public administration in no way guarantees a seat on the council. More than one college-educated candidate for office has been defeated by a high-school dropout.

This tribe, like so many others, faces multiple problems of resource development and the delivery of social services to the tribal members. Resource development requires understanding and negotiating extensive sophisticated contracts with national corporations who want to do business on the reservation. The council relies heavily upon the Bureau of Indian Affairs or outside consultants for technical advice because so few members are college educated. Some consultants used by the council are Indians, but most are not. In the past, council members have been poorly informed by white consultants and the Bureau of Indian Affairs, so when they feel uneasy about the lack of information they have, with which they often table the decision, which is an Indian way of making a decision.

A large housing project was built on the reservation about a mile from the tribal office. This program is sufficiently flexible, so that one can either rent or purchase a home, with payments based upon income. These HUD units were designed with three or more bedrooms and large front and back lots to accommodate extended Indian families. An additional hundred units are planned by the tribe to house a growing Indian population. The reservation uses the label *housing development* to refer to these subsidized homes, but in Madison, citizens use the purgative term *housing project* when they refer to them. Facing the tribal office about a block away are about fifty houses, some mobile, for federal employees at the hospital and for tribal members who work on or near the tribal office. Some live there even though they do not work on the reservation, because they moved in decades ago.

Up until perhaps a couple of decades ago, most of the tribal members lived off the land, far away from each other. Today, many Indians are living in close proximity to one another. This often results in disputes within the housing units, in the tribal office, and in other public facilities. There is a discerned need for rules and regulations to reduce conflict that has come about because of crowding. The Bureau of Indian Affairs originally designed these housing units to minimize the cost of providing electricity, sewage, and water and completely overlooked the cultural reality that the Indians prefer distance between neighbors.

Virtually all of the federal programs formerly operated by the Bureau of Indian Affairs for the tribe are now being operated by the tribe. This new-found economic stability has served as a magnet for professional tribal members to return to the reservation. The tribal council is aggressively seeking housing funds in order to attract (and retain) college-educated tribal members back to the reservation. This reservation has more college-educated tribal members than most, and most of them would rather live and work at home than in the cities.

More than a river separates the town from the reservation. It is a formidable chasm that few on either side of the river have attempted to gulf. Even though 80 percent of the students attending public school in Madison come from the reservation, only one faculty member has ever attended the annual reservation pow wow. None of the faculty have ever visited the reservation, so for them, it is foreign and alien territory. At the entry to the reservation, there is a sign that tells you that you are entering an Indian reservation.

The sign is unnecessary. Dried up earth surrounds the houses and tribal buildings. Water is not used for flowers or grass.

The small restaurant on the reservation serves fresh food and homemade soup and sandwiches. There is an ice-cream fountain which attracts the children to its door all day long. It is clean, and although the prices are more modest than those in Madison, it is rare to see a non-Indian in the place. In spite of the steady stream of traffic into the restaurant, no one is in a hurry, and the slow service gives diners an opportunity to visit with others. Here, as in Madison, everyone knows one another, but unlike in Madison, everyone is also related. The restaurant serves as a center for catching up on the gossip of the day. It does not have a liquor license. Wine and beer can be purchased at the grocery store next door, but the tribe draws the line at hard liquor.

A tribal community college on the reservation provides remedial coursework to qualify students for the state university system and offers a number of Associate of Arts degrees. Some students take one or two courses, others take a full degree program. Typing, data processing, word processing, culture, and art courses are in great demand. In addition, the community college functions as a center for job training. It has offered courses in agriculture and industry, particularly welding. The college administration would like to offer a wider variety of programs, but it is limited by funding, and the facility itself is small and inadequate for a community college. However, interaction between faculty and students is high, and because of the few decision makers, administrators can quickly make curriculum changes when appropriate. The community college is run separately from the tribal Department of Education.

The tribal Education Department commissioned a survey to ascertain the educational interests of its members. The first part of the needs assessment focused on a profile of the members, which found that the average age was thirty for males, twenty-seven for females; one-third were married; two-thirds were single; single parents, or divorced; and, of those living on the reservation, one-quarter of the population were either unenrolled or enrolled members of another tribe. Four-fifths of the respondents went to a rural school locally or an Indian school on or off the reservation. One-third of the male population and four-fifths of the female population completed high school. Of those who completed high school, one-third went to an urban high school, one-third to a rural high school, and one-third to a BIA boarding school.

Of the females who completed high school, two-thirds reported that their training was sufficient for college preparation, but only one-half of the males felt the training they received was sufficient for college preparation.

Of the females, 50 percent had vocational training after leaving high school, while none of the males had vocational training. Of the females, 15 percent had taken part in a federal/state education program, while none of the males participated in a federally subsidized program. Of the females, 15 percent graduated with an Associate of Arts degree, while none of the males did.

Half of the respondents went to a four-year degree program in the ratio of 1:3 male-female. Of those who went to a four-year degree program, 75 percent majored in business or computer science. Two-thirds of the males and all of the females reported the education they received was useful. Two-thirds of the males and all of the females who went through post–high-school or college training reported that they were working at jobs for which they were trained.

When asked what grade level they desired to achieve, one-sixth of the males said a G.E.D. level and one-sixth wanted to go to graduate school, and two-thirds of the females desired a four-year college degree, and one-third wanted to attend graduate school.

Despite the fact that few Indians want to relocate, and there are only a handful of computer-oriented positions available either on the reservation or in Madison, the overwhelming majority in the survey listed computers and business as the areas they wanted to specialize in at the college.

The tribal council administers many of the social, education, and economic-development programs one would find in any municipality. Health programs range from prenatal care to senior citizen programs. The hospital is local, it is open twenty-four hours a day, and it provides at least the basic health care for the most prevalent health programs, which on the reservation are diabetes, childhood diseases, alcoholism, and geriatrics. Health education and prevention includes providing daily aerobic exercise in the tribal swimming pool. The Reagan budget cuts seriously undermined the pool usage, because the tribe found itself without funds for maintenance and swimming instructors.

The tribal council has considerable power over the lives of the reservation Indians. Every election causes a power shift and changes in tribal program employment. Job security is more dependent upon being in the good graces of the incumbents than with job performance. The tribe does have personnel procedures to force equity in hiring and firing practices, but the tribal council maintains the final say in all matters under its jurisdiction. This places program managers in difficult positions from time to time.

A few years ago, the tribal council recruited one of its members who had graduated from a prestigious university to head up the tribal Department of Education. She had been well trained and had established an excellent reputation as an Indian educator. But the council agreed only to a annual contract, sending a message to her staff that whatever changes she demanded could be temporary or disregarded altogether. She worked long and hard to bring about more productivity in all the programs, only to find that she could not hire or fire people under her without the permission of the tribal council. While she was able to make considerable progress during the year she was there, it was no where near the first-rate department she could have built had she been given the authority to reward and sanction her staff and to exercise control over the education budget.

Tribes sometimes find themselves in a fiscal "catch 22." Programs are funded in different federal cycles. For instance, the tribe can be informed in July that funding for an economic-development project will be available before the end of the year, but they also must hire and gear up for this same program beginning in the normal October 1 fiscal year. They must spend money in order to receive funds retroactively. If the "start-up" funds are not available, other tribal programs are raided (and returned later) in order to begin; but that also means project managers are never certain about their budgets.

Education programs are always a hot seat on any reservation. Money is allocated for college, admission to Indian schools, curriculum development, special job-training programs, and unique demonstration programs for primary and secondary schools. Generally speaking, there are more college graduates and graduates of masters and doctorate programs in education than in other fields. This is true for the reservation near Madison. Indians are leaving the traditional occupations of farming and ranching because of the formidable expense and necessity of automation and because the population is increasing, placing more demands on tribal lands for homes than for grazing.

The health and human service sector of the reservation experiences minimal conflict with the tribal council because skilled health professionals are in short supply. Most of the medical staff and paraprofessional staff working at the health center are not Indians, although the ratio of Indian to non-Indian employment pattern is changing. The exception in health services is the alcoholism program. The entire staff is Indian.

The alcoholism program is run efficiently, because all of the staff were former alcoholics and come from this reservation. People working in the tribal office willingly pay a dollar or two for lunch at the center, because the cook is one of the best on the reservation and the meals are delicious. The money that is made at the center goes to support the program. However, the cure rate is about average for any alcoholism center in the country.

A major change over the decade has been a greater emphasis in educating young children before they begin drinking. The reservation has a teen al-anon program. Because everyone knows everyone on the reservation, they work with entire families when one member is in the center. The main problem they have is finding work for people after they leave. Boredom is a recovering alcoholic's worst enemy. Without some meaningful activity many return to alcoholism.

The gymnasium buzzes with activity from dawn till dusk. People spend a part of the day in the indoor swimming pool (when funds permit repair and staffing), cafeteria, and a multipurpose room that is used for meetings. Programs are established for children and adults and include aquatics for weight control and recreational swimming for adults.

There is one other building, the tribal police office. Most disputes are handled there and in tribal court. The tribal court is appointed by the tribal council, so when a dispute arises that involves the tribal council and a tribal member, it is evident that the balance of power lies within the tribal council member. However, there is at least a sincere attempt to adjudicate disputes reasonably.

The tribal court knows the families involved and tends to handle matters from a personal rather than a legal framework. From time to time, accusations are made that tribal courts do not function as professionally as they should. Although there is a written legal code, there is more leeway in a tribal court than in the county or state court. In spite of accusations, few tribal members want the tribal court to be a replica of non-Indian court systems, precisely because it is "in-house" or "family."

The tribal court also exercises jurisdiction over Indian child welfare cases, on or off the reservation. Unfortunately, functioning at optimal or even reasonable levels is severely curtailed by the lack of funds to hire professional social workers who can assess family situations.

The tribe also runs a group home away from the center of the reservation. This facility is for adolescents who are out of control, who have been persistent truants, who have drug or alcohol problems, and whose home life is considered inappropriate by the tribal court. Unfortunately, this too runs into funding problems because the facility is inadequate to handle the volume of youngsters in need of care.

The Ethos

The term *ethos* is used here to describe a value system governing collective behavior which regulates societal religious, family, economic, and political norms. The purpose of an ethos or value system is for societal survival. Values gain their legitimacy through norms, roles, and institutions.[2] While values regulate collective behavior, individuals can and often do deviate to the left or right of the center. In fact, the center represents the absolute acquiescence to all the rules, at all times, and in every way, which in fact does not exist. No one, we are told, is perfect.

How do we internalize a value system? Childhood rearing gives us our first understanding of right and wrong, of what society expects from us, and appropriate behavior towards society. These are "norms." Roles arise organically from norms and establish our place within societal economic, social, and political institutions. From these, society creates institutions, such as those of education and government, that serve to integrate individuals within a social milieu, and establish the training, bureaucracy, and generally agreed upon rules of the rites of passage.

Cultures evolve, but changes in value systems may take centuries to even be noticed.[3] Although people perceive that cultures change (as Charlie Hill says "seen a Pilgrim lately"?) they are confusing the norms, roles, and institutions in a society with the values that remain constant. Changes in collective norms occur when cultural lifestyles move from a hunter-gatherer society into agricultural, industrial, and postindustrial/technological society. In other words, collective behavior adapts to changes in technology, without changing the basic ethos or value system. The townspeople of Madison and the tribal members on the reservation have separate and distinctly different value systems. That is not to say that the cultures are so divergent that detente is not feasible. It is to say that they may view the same reality through different prisms.

The ethos of a tribal society are distinctly different from those of a nontribal society. The following analysis carries with it a caveat that societies have a range of differences because individuals are different (see table 5.1). They represent what Max Weber termed the "ideal" which does not actually exist but functions as a societal goal.

The Indian ethos is derived from a common understanding

Table 5.1 A Comparative Ethos of Tribal and Nontribal Cultures

	Tribal Society	Nontribal Society
Values	Man collaborates with the natural environment.	Man manipulates the natural environment.
Norms	Characteristics supportive of cooperative behavior.	Characteristics supportive of competitive behavior.
Roles	Charismatic based upon individual influence. Power is vested in the person.	Bureaucratic based upon explicit set of rules. Power is vested in the position one holds.
Institutions	Supportive of cooperation.	Supportive of competition.

that sharing, generosity, and thinking as a group rather than as an individual contribute significantly to tribal survival. That is not to say that all Indians are generous, cooperative, and altruistic, but it is to say that the ideal (which does not really exist in any society) is for people to think of the common good, or a narrowing between the haves and the have nots. The European-American ethos values independence, individualism, a social and economic distancing from the have nots, and a work ethic aimed at wealth. Indians who lack education but are generally personable and get along with other members are often placed in positions of power and trust.

White society requires credentials such as a college degree in order to earn a role as a leader. It has set up a bureaucratic structure, a rite of passage institutionalized through the education system, matured with experience, and a track record of sound business judgments. With this background, some will emerge into positions of power.

Of course, the distance between reality or the way people actually behave and the ideal, the way they are supposed to behave, can be confusing. Indians do not live in a vacuum, and they can see and are schooled into knowing how the rest of society lives. Sometimes their behavior is no different than that of white Americans. But Indians are different. Even today, Indians think of themselves as Navajo, or Cherokee, or Sioux, and then as American, a sharp contrast with the white citizens of Madison. Many of the residents of Madison have blurred cultural backgrounds and do not identify themselves as German Americans or Swedish Americans, only Americans.

Holidays provide a good example of the differing values of these two cultures. Both cultures celebrate Thanksgiving Day. Both buy turkey and watch the Macy's parade on television. But Madison residents regard Thanksgiving Day as a symbol of earning the right to exist in America through hard work and thrift, a celebration of the American dream. This symbol is institutionalized in the school classrooms during November. In school the children learn about how the pilgrims, Puritans, and Indians sat down together at a table with a prayer for deliverance from famine. Indians see Thanksgiving Day as an invasion of their homeland, Indian generosity rewarded with death, famine, and destruction.

Fourth of July firecrackers can be heard on the reservation and in the town. For the townspeople, July 4 means picnics, barbecues, and symbolically a celebration of their country. The Indians see July 4 as a day of feasting like anyone else, but the symbolism of winning a revolutionary war is lost on a people who are struggling even today to gain their independence and their homeland.

Separate cultures, different perspectives of history, and the future have made strange bedfellows of the residents of Madison and the tribal members. Each secretly wishes the other would go away, but like the conflicted people in Ireland or Israel and Palestine, they are inextricably woven together, dependent upon one another by geography, history, and most important, economics.

A healthy source of income in Madison is derived from the federal dollars that flow into the reservation. Without these funds, even the small stores would go out of business. The local branch bank could not stay in business without the tribal accounts. However, the tribe does not have the economic infrastructure to support an appliance store, a newspaper, a bank, or a gas station. The tribe is dependent upon Madison for all the small items necessary to finance a home or own a car.

Interdependence has a battleground, the classroom. Each of these cultures wants education to reflect its cultural values. The town has fought to maintain control over education. With each generation it loses more youth to the cities. The reservation is also locked into battle. Its population is increasing, and greater numbers of educated Indians are returning as the council develops programs requiring special skills. For both of these cultures, the shaping of the Madison school system is the key to viable growth and development, concomitant with a comfortable rural lifestyle.

The important question is whether the same school can respond to the different needs of different cultures, or is institutional racism so deeply imbedded in the community that the local public school system cannot or will not educate both cultures equitably?

6

Community Perceptions of the Madison K through Twelve Public School System

Both the town and the reservation community had strong feelings about the Madison school system, the focal point of the Madison evaluation. Each waved the banner of "community control" as a century of uneasy peace between the town and reservation came to a thundering halt. The town of Madison defined community control in terms of geography, whereas the reservation defined it in terms of student population. Each definition legitimately describes community control.[1] At the time of the Madison evaluation, both the town and the reservation were adamant that only one definition should prevail. The underlying rationale for this uncompromising position lay in the different perspectives each community had of the Madison school system.

The Town

The Madison High School has a long narrow hallway displaying pictures of graduating seniors. The photographs taken during the forties and fifties visibly broadcast sporadic Indian enrollment. In more recent picture, the triumphant smiling faces take on a new patina. Each succeeding year shows that the racial makeup of the Madison school has changed, until recently when white students are in the minority and Indians from the reservation, the majority. The 340 K through twelve student body has an enrollment of 270 Indians.

Madison residents are loyal and staunch alumni. The school was built by their grandparents and graduated their parents. Loyalty can be easily understood, because the Madison system represents more than bricks and books; it also represents intergenerational continuity. The school buildings have not kept pace with time, and a once-vital system that proudly sent alumni to the state university has been losing ground physically and educationally for fifteen years. With all of the problems besetting the school, loyalty to it remains undaunted. It is a school filled with childhood memories.

Madison faculty and citizens attribute the downward trend in scholastic achievement to the new student body, the Indians. The Indian students once attended Indian school exclusively, but since the seventies they have been entering public school. Today they are more likely to be in the public school system at Madison than in the BIA system.

For more than a decade, teacher retention has been on the decline because fewer recruits actually come from Madison or the surrounding rural areas. Many of the senior faculty were brought up in ranching and farming, went away to college, and returned to secure a teaching position and a stable income. In some years, a 50 percent teacher turnover, especially of new teachers, is not unusual.

There was a new school superintendent every year for ten years. The present one has lasted three years, but the school principals, both at the elementary and at the high school have been fired. Although the faculty and administrative turnover is unusually high even for a rural community, the school represents jobs for residents whose family farms no longer sustain them. In an economically depressed area, that is the only security they have. Maintaining the status quo means being able to pay the mortgage.

Remodeling or repair to the school creates jobs for the Madison locals. Second only to the tribal accounts, the school generates business with the local bank, grocery store, diner, restaurant, general store, and even the newspaper. Bus drivers who take the students to neighboring towns for athletic competitions, the school nurse, the cafeteria cooks and servers are dependent upon the paycheck they receive from the Madison school system.

Residents are aware that the system has run-down buildings and that scholastically all children function at lower levels than those in neighboring towns, but alumni loyalty and job security make them fiercely determined to resist any change threatening local control.

This fierce determination extends to the members of the school board, who are responsible for the hiring and firing of all school personnel. They are aggressive and vigilant in maintaining control, even to the extent of hiring teachers directly instead of delegating that responsibility to the school superintendent (although his recommendations carry weight with the board).

Teachers often resign from the Madison school because they prefer to live and work in a less isolated community. There are at least half a dozen Indian educators with Master's degrees on the reservation who want to work and live in the area. This human resource pool would contribute significantly to the stability of the teaching staff. In spite of the 50 percent annual turnover rate, only one Indian has been hired, aside from the one who runs the Title 4 Indian Education Act project. The present faculty of sixty (K–12) has one Indian professional teacher, a couple of Indian teacher aides, an Indian bus driver, and an Indian truant officer. The school administration, from principals to counselors, are all non-Indian. The school board members maintain that they cannot find any qualified Indians for faculty positions.

When the school came up for renewal of accreditation in the early 1980s, shock waves were felt throughout the town. The Madison system failed accreditation. However, it was given time to fix whatever was necessary.

The accreditation team concentrated on the physical plant and teacher certification for the grades they were teaching. The fear that the school would lose state and federal revenue mobilized the Madison community into action. The power elite in the town and school focused on remedies addressing the issues raised by the accreditation board. Teachers were shuffled around to teach classes they were certified to teach. The kitchen was cleaned, and the physical plant received a coat of paint. Little attention was paid to the educational deterioration of the school. This became the battle cry of the newly created Indian Parent Advisory Board. Their voices could only be ignored for so long, because Madison had applied for and received funding under Impact Aid to subsidize the system for a spiraling Indian student enrollment. One provision for receiving these funds under Impact Aid was the formation of an Indian Advisory Board.

The Madison School Board members were on the proverbial horns of a dilemma. The choices before them were to increase local taxes to bring the school buildings within state standards or to apply for federal funds and open the door to Indian governing participation. Raising additional taxes in a dwindling population would almost certainly produce opposition by the town residents and might increase flight from the rural community. However, introducing any change that included Indian participation was aggressively opposed by the power elite. Administrators, faculty, and all those who had a financial vested interest united under the banner of community control. For a while, community control was maintained through the election process. Those eligible to vote for the school board were residents of Madison, and the voting districts were gerrymandered so that the few Indian residents of Madison could not muster a majority to select a member.

The Indians first filed a complaint with the Civil Rights Commission, arguing that their children were the majority in the student body but gerrymandering prevented Indian representation on the school board. This complaint was heard, but did not bring any results.

Madison was just settling back from that confrontation when the Indians filed another complaint with the Department of Education. At the same time, they held meetings on the reservation to begin a feasibility study to build and operate a tribal school with the Impact Aid and other federal funds currently distributed to the Madison public school system.

This was not a idle threat. In 1985, $1,200,000 of federal Indian money had come to the school. In addition, Madison was due to receive federal Impact Aid for building a new high school in 1986. Madison residents now had more difficult choices to make. Either increase taxes to build a new high school and support faculty salaries without Indian money, or adjust to sharing governance with the Indian population. Furthermore, if their existing schools did not meet state standards, and the Indians built a new school on the reservation, many of the Madison children would have to attend school on the reservation.

Battle lines were drawn, and some even threatened to send their children to a high school thirty miles away rather than have them attend school on the reservation. That is until 1985, when an Indian living in Madison and working for the tribe ran for a position on the school board. For the first time in its history, the Madison School Board had an Indian member.

The election was heated, but the Indians voted for an Indian college graduate who worked on the reservation. Non-Indians also voted for him, in the belief that accommodation was necessary in order to maintain the Madison school system within the town. It is interesting to note that the Indian was the only college graduate on the school board.

One persuasive argument was his support of building the new high school in the town of Madison rather than on the reservation. Not that he would not have liked to have the school built on the reservation, but the reality was that as a result of a survey conducted on the reservation a year before, support for a tribal school did not carry a majority on the reservation.

The School Administrators

The school board in Madison retains all of the power to hire, fire, sanction, and reward. It is an elected body, comprising five members that up till 1986 were exclusively white. With the exception of the American Indian who is a college graduate and works on the reservation, school board members have all been business men, high-school graduates, and alumni of the Madison system. All budgetary and personnel decisions, even minute ones, are carried out by the school board.

As a general rule, the board accepted recommendations from the school superintendent. However, in the past decade, they had displayed minimal disposition to delegating either budgetary or personnel authority to the superintendent. It can be argued that this reluctance was a reflection of the yearly turnover of the superintendent position. Or it can be argued that withholding authority normally relegated to a superintendent created a chain of events leading to the annual turnover.

This game of musical chairs had a profound impact on education in Madison. Teachers who had been in the system for fifteen to twenty years were well aware of the chain of command written into the school code. Nonetheless, whenever there was disagreement between teachers and administrators, teachers formally or informally appealed to the school board. This behavior permitted them to ignore or circumvent administrative decisions. The school board treated school administrators as outsiders and school teachers as community. Consequently, the school administration was wary of providing the proactive leadership this system needed because unpopular decisions were sometimes reversed by the school board upon complaints filed by teachers.

At the time of the Madison evaluation, the school superintendent had held his position for two years (1985–1987). Inasmuch as he was the eighth school superintendent in ten years, he held the record for survival. He needed to last one more year to attain tenure. He was not a creative or innovative educator, but he was a good

administrator, careful with the budget, even tight-fisted, and persuaded federal authorities to authorize Impact Act to fund a new
high school. This brought new money into the town of Madison
and jobs for those in the building trades. The building was scheduled
to be completed in 1987.

He understood that creating an environment for educational
excellence required recruitment of innovative and creative leadership in the principal positions. In his position as superintendent he
displayed the same wariness as the school board to delegate authority that ordinarily goes with the position of principal. His principals
were required to receive permission from him for everyday decisions
such as scheduling, in-service training, or the purchase of any item
over two hundred dollars. Neither principal knew the dollar amount
of any line item in his or her budget.

The Madison system was in turmoil because the superintendent had forced the resignation of the high-school principal after
less than a year in the position and requested the resignation of
the grammar-school principal. The grammar-school principal had
not been as accommodating as the high-school principal. He refused
to hand in his resignation and planned on filing a grievance with
the school board and state education authorities, and a civil law
suit both against the school superintendent and against the school
board. The school board decided to back up the superintendent,
possibly out of weariness with the annual hunt for a new superintendent. But the members were also wary of his growing independence.

The newest member of the school board, the American Indian,
provided the swing vote for the superintendent's tenure. It is ironic
because during a board meeting prior to the election of the Indian,
the superintendent had raised objections against using Impact Aid
money to teach an Indian class that the 874 Indian Parent Advisory
board wanted. He stated that use of funds should benefit all students,
not just Indians, and that non-Indian students would not benefit
from an Indian cultural class. His political survival antenna led
him to reverse that decision. The Indian Parent Advisory Board
emerged into a power player in the Madison community. They
were responsible for petitioning the Civil Rights Commission, filing
complaints with the Office of Education and forcing the entire system to a comprehensive outside evaluation.

The grade-school principal began employment in Madison
after more than two decades in education. He appeared to be well
organized, and though he had worked in the community for only
two years, he was well informed about community happenings. It
was difficult to gauge his real capabilities as an educational leader

in this system, since most of the decision making was out of his control. One clue to his competency was the way he approached the annual teacher evaluation. The Madison Teachers Union designed the evaluation instrument. The school principal reported a lack of knowledge about measuring instructional goals for each grade under his jurisdiction, so he relegated the teaching evaluation process to the teachers. He reported that the evaluation instrument needed improvement, but he himself did not know how to improve it. He attended conferences to learn what he termed "the state of the art" in education.

His teachers did not vest much trust in him. They were conditioned to having a new principal each year and knew that their positions depended more upon access to the school board than pleasing the principal. They also complained of his inconsistent behavior which fluctuated between being authoritarian and being passive.

He was in an emotional and professional wringer. When he came to Madison, he knew it would be his last position before retiring within the state retirement pension plan. He was aware that his predecessors had lasted one, sometimes two, years, and he needed three years for tenure and full pension upon retirement. At the time of the study, he had completed two years. He also knew that the superintendent wanted him replaced. Any move in that direction would most certainly jeopardize his pension, and he planned court action if the superintendent or school board fired him.

He displayed a macho bravado in conversation, but was careful not to allow his personality to antagonize the teaching staff. He was well aware of the power of the senior teaching staff in the Madison system, and he did not want to confront them. He had tried to build what he termed "team spirit" among the faculty, and to govern by consensus. His fear of jeopardizing his pension, his lack of knowledge about instructional objectives for each grade, and concern over the influence teachers had with the school board placed constraints on whatever role he might have had as an educational leader.

He expressed great optimism about the potential Madison had for becoming an excellent school system within five years. He expressed an interest in hiring American Indian teachers but was quick to proclaim that these decisions were not his to make. He related that an American Indian candidate for a faculty position had come to Madison and had turned down the job offered because of an incident at a local business establishment which the candidate took to be a racial slur. He felt it was difficult to recruit American Indians to Madison, but he would continue to try. Given his tenuous position, it was doubtful that he would use whatever little influence he had to recruit or advocate for Indian faculty at the grammar school.

The principal related that all of the teachers were certified and taught in their area of certification. He was aware of the inadequacy of the two-hour kindergarten program but reiterated that that decision was not his. He reported that team spirit was building, although the year before one-fourth of his teaching staff had resigned. The teaching staff had come to him with a request for a multipurpose room, which he felt was educationally sound but lacked support from the superintendent or the school board because of the expense involved. He reported a problem with student discipline but did not think the new school policy of suspension to control deviant behavior was an adequate solution.

He had a number of confrontations with parents in the community, particularly the American Indian parents. With his second year almost completed, he reported a better understanding of some of the issues than when he had first come to Madison. The main complaints from the parents concerned his heavy-handed approach without investigating the causes of why children act out.

In a system where the principal had very little authority, his role was to resolve conflicts and schedule classes and events rather than to be an initiator of policy and procedures. He had not assessed the quality of the library collection or education in the Madison grammar school but was proud of that fact that he was instrumental in getting the school kitchen up to accreditation standards.

The high-school principal had come to Madison with almost fifteen years of service in a major city system. Her previous position was as department head of the school counseling center, and she took the Madison position as a step up on the administrative ladder. Unfortunately, she was hired by the school board against the wishes of the superintendent, who had backed a candidate that he had worked with previously. From her arrival, she experienced conflict with the superintendent. His office was next to hers, and she was under his constant scrutiny. Within months of her arrival, he requested and received her resignation, effective at the end of the school year. She reported that he had difficulty working with assertive women and that the effort it would take to remain in her position was simply not worth it to her. She returned to her old school.

The Reservation

The reservation's commitment to education had a long history. In the days when few Indians attended college, Indians from this reservation were well represented in the state's and nation's universities including the prestigious Ivy League. So when the seventies produced fewer and fewer Indians capable of entering higher education, concern escalated, and four community studies were conducted between 1984 and 1987 to get at the bottom of the downward trend. The first study was an informal needs assessment of the public school in Madison. The discussion during the next tribal meeting arrived at a consensus that the school should include tribally relevant teaching materials and improve the physical plant, busing, and cafeteria food. Concern was also expressed about the indifference of the teaching staff and about the families and homes of the reservation students. A second survey profiled the educational attainment and aspirations of tribal members. Two others focused on whether the tribe wanted to build its own tribal school.

Each survey seemed to elicit more and more frustration with education in general and Madison in particular. The first survey findings were reported to Madison, but were ignored. The second was a needs assessment commissioned by the tribal college to plan programs and courses in conjunction with the educational levels and aspirations of tribal members. It became evident from this report that some tribal members required remedial high-school work in order to qualify for college-level programs. By the time the third survey was conducted, it was evident that Madison was not responding to the first survey, which identified the absence of culturally relevant curriculum. This they felt was directly related to the lack of meaningful Indian participation in spite of the newly formed Indian Parent Advisory Committee. The Indians asserted that the Madison system treated their role in governance of Indian entitlements as perfunctory.

One agreed-upon premise was that the federal government would fund the building of a new high school under Impact Aid, either in Madison or on the reservation. Four options were laid out. The first option was to create a new public school district on the reservation. The second was to build a tribal high school adjacent to an existing reservation primary school at Sweetgrass, where most of the traditionals sent their children. The third was to create a new Indian-controlled school at the center of the reservation. The fourth option was for the tribe to work cooperatively with the Madison School Board.

There was a 26 percent return of the survey instrument. Most of the Indians (90 percent) felt they should work cooperatively with the Madison School Board to improve the system. Failing any progress in that direction, 60 percent said the tribe should create a new reservation school district. Twenty percent wanted a high school attached to the Sweetgrass primary school.

One interpretation of the high positive response to working with the Madison public system was anxiety that a reservation high school opened up the potential for education to be as immersed in tribal politics as is the tribal Department of Education. Tribal members evidently felt that in time, the sheer numbers of Indian children in the Madison school system would bring about changes in school governance, curriculum, and faculty sensitivity they desired. Others thought rocking the boat might set race relations between the town and reservation back to the fifties.

In 1985 a formalized study was conducted on the reservation. The results were congruent with the first community meeting held two years earlier. The priorities listed were also consistent. The Indians wanted culturally relevant activities with Indian language heading the top of the list, a greater emphasis on physical activities such as swimming and competitive sports, and more field trips (which is especially important in an isolated rural area).

All of the surveys indicated that Indians perceived the Madison school system as poor to average but were optimistic about working with and for the system to make it better. They had reasons for this optimism. The Office of Education had conducted a study of the Madison system and brought pressure on the town to accept the necessary changes. Within a year after the first Indian board member was elected, another ran for and won election. Now there were two Indians on the five-member school board.

Summary

Madison residents had a vested interest in the Madison system because it represented intergenerational continuity and the only stable source of jobs. For them, community control was opposing any erosion of the status quo that meant including the Indian presence in staffing or curriculum, even though the school faced physical and educational decline.

The reservation also had a vested interest in the Madison school. In spite of Indian education entitlement subsidies that largely supported the school, there had been a decline of college-bound Indian students who graduated from the Madison system. For them, community control meant accommodating the needs of Indian students representing 70 percent of the student body.

It is likely that the status quo would have prevailed except for the financial crunch Madison would have faced without the Indian education subsidies, which was a real possibility if the Indians had petitioned to build a school system on the reservation, and considering the assertive stand taken initially by the Indian Parents Advisory Committee. Through them, both the tribe and the federal government began taking an active interest in the governance of the Madison school system.

7

The Madison Study: Classroom Evaluations K through Four

The Department of Education procrastinated investigating the substance of charges filed by the Indian Parents Advisory Committee against Madison. After years of written inquiries, in 1986 it sent a field investigator to Madison. The complaints were found to be valid, and the field investigator reported that the Indian Parents Advisory Committee members were not participants in the planning, development, and monitoring of the Indian-funded school programs. The Madison school system was out of compliance with the spirit and the intent of the regulatory provisions of P.L. 81–874.

The school board fired back with documentation of tribal council sign-offs of the annual Madison district request for the 81–874 entitlements. The Indian committee replied that tribal authorization was obtained without knowledge of the line item breakdown, or inclusion of the Parent Advisory Committee recommendations, prerequisites of meaningful negotiations between the tribal council and the school board. In addition, they lodged a complaint of gerrymandering effectively locking out Indian representation on the school board.

The U.S. Department of Education (DOE) report found that the town of Madison had gerrymandered the district so that the areas of greatest concentration of Indian population were divided into several voting districts, with insufficient numbers in any single one to win election to the school board. In addition, the parents of students living within the reservation were excluded from representation on the school board. They were, technically speaking, outside of the Madison district boundaries, even though most of the entitlement funds were generated from students living on the reservation.

The DOE report stated that "an attitudinal change on the part of the District officials will be essential." The Madison School Board interpreted this as a thinly veiled threat, not to be taken lightly. Compounding their problems, the Regional Accreditation Association concluded that Madison was not up to standards of accreditation. The combination of the DOE report and the accreditation evaluation played a major role in the election of an Indian to the school board that year, mainly through non-Indian voters living within the district who became worried about property tax increases should the federal Indian education entitlement be withdrawn. When the Indian member of the school board was seated, the first recommendation he made was to conduct a comprehensive evaluation of the school system. The recommendation was passed, and an evaluation was conducted.

Various community representatives expressed concern about the evaluation research methodology. In an effort to reduce tension, the evaluators held extensive open discussions with administrators, faculty, and community. The faculty were apprehensive that Madison would compare unfavorably with large city systems or even other rural schools with a homogeneous population. They felt that a fairer assessment would be a comparison of Madison with an Indian-controlled school since the student population was predominantly Indian. But this was rejected on the grounds that Indian-controlled schools have only a ten-year history and a limited funding base to acquire capital resources, whereas public schools receive state, federal, and local funding and have been operating for at least fifty years.

In the end, an agreement was reached that a fair assessment would be a comparison of Madison to other schools within the state, since most were as rural as Madison. The evaluation methodology would include in-class observations; a survey of the textbooks and interviews with staff, faculty, and administrators; and a community assessment. The comprehensive focus permitted an impartial and thorough measurement of the school system. Everyone concerned knew this evaluation was politically volatile and expressed a hope that a cooperative effort of school, town, and reservation would serve as the working foundation for change.

An Evaluator's Perspective

School evaluations are never completely divorced from bias. The selection, or selecting out, of different factors is the result of a personal philosophy of education. Here is mine.

I have seen students who ace an exam but cannot write a paper or conduct a reasonable level of research on any topic. I remember a student years ago at the Pierre Indian School who could not read or write at the fifth-grade level but had acquired college-level knowledge of astronomy. How this student acquired this knowledge without the aid of sufficient reading skills will always be a mystery to me. Then the leading questions are how do children learn, under what conditions do they retain knowledge, and how do they go beyond the classroom to generalize a gestalt about the world?

Designing concrete scales for learning can be a humbling experience, because children learn in spite of poor teaching, and conversely learning can elude students in spite of excellent teaching. But there is one aspect of education that seems, at least for me, to account for some children flourishing and others floundering in spite of any system they are in. It is called the "Pygmalion effect," described beautifully by Rosenthal.[1]

A thumbnail description of this phenomenon says that children succeed because a school system, or a significant person in the system, says to them that they can learn, they are intelligent and worthwhile, and that the challenge of learning is within their intellectual grasp. Someone ignites a spark within that child, and he or she acquires a sense of capability and self-esteem in spite of being surrounded by negative forces.

I have watched children fail year after year. Some, even after years of failure and tuning out in the classroom, retain that spark, that inner confidence in their own self-worth. They persist until eventually the right teacher ignites their thirst for knowledge. Then the class zombie becomes a sponge, absorbing what was lost years before and connecting to what is going on in the class.

The system that we are about to dissect is like many in this country. It does not have adequate facilities, teaching skills, of books, and it is miles away from educational resources. Americans have knee-jerk responses from time to time about prioritizing spending billions on defense and a fraction of the federal budget on education. But in the long run they will vote with their pocketbook, and systems like this are left to struggle without the necessary requisites to instill quality education. Older teachers have seen promises of change come and go, and newer teachers become demoralized by the contagious apathy of the old-timers.

Nonetheless, some children will rise above an inadequate educational system. It is with this realization that it becomes clear that an evaluation is not the SRA scores achieved by students, but rather the message these children receive from a system that either sets sparks within them or chills their desire to learn. From my perspective, learning environment and expectations play a far more significant role than any other factor in student achievement. For this reason, the evaluation of the Madison system includes teacher expectation and classroom environment.

I and two colleagues conducted the reservation and the community surveys. One lived and worked on the reservation as director of Tribal Education, the other was highly experienced in conducting Indian sociological surveys. As principal investigator, I complied and incorporated their raw data into this report.

Except for the first four grades, several teachers are responsible for classroom learning in each grade and each subject. The reform in education of the sixties led to two trends, which in my opinion have seriously undermined education. One was moving students away from their school district to larger systems. This makes accountability more difficult and, in many cases, impossible. In large systems, the most educationally vulnerable can get lost. Centralization was considered necessary in order to effect desegregation and/or for economic efficiency, but in solving one educational problem, we have opened a Pandora's box to others with far more serious consequences.

The middle school became a by-product of consolidated local systems. Where at one time a primary school, grades kindergarten through eight, was held accountable for its final product, dividing educational levels permitted sending problem learners to the next level, with some sort of mystical dream that the learning difficulties would resolve themselves with maturation in junior high, or from junior high, to high school.

The school system under discussion was artificially divided into three levels, with the junior high in the high-school building, separated by a hall. Logically, a three-tier school arrangement does not make sense because of the small student population. However, it did make it easy for each level to blame the preceding level for student deficiencies. This evaluation ignored the three-tier system and divided up the grades by teacher responsibilities. That is, through the fourth grade, single teachers were responsible for their classes in all subjects. Grades five through twelve were departmentalized.

The main handicap to evaluating these grades was the departmentalization, especially in the middle school, which led to evaluating the same teacher twice because she/he taught two different grades at the same time in the same classroom. This happens in rural schools, but it has been a long time since the one-room school house was the norm, and teacher education no longer prepares teachers to handle two levels of the same subject at the same time and in the same classroom.

Student Achievement Tests

The Madison school and the state used the Scholastic Research Associates (SRA) as a measurement of achievement (see table 7.1). Although this measurement was not used exclusively in every school

Table 7.1 SRA Scores for Grades K through 4

	FIRST GRADE Madison	State
Reading	1.8	2.3
	SECOND GRADE Madison	State
Reading	3.4	4.0
Math	3.0	3.5
	THIRD GRADE Madison	State
Reading	4.2	5.1
Math	4.0	4.7
Language Arts	4.0	4.7
	FOURTH GRADE Madison	State
Reading	5.7	6.1
Math	5.5	5.6
Language Arts	6.1	5.7
Social Studies	6.2	6.2
Science	6.3	6.3

district within the state, the state itself used SRA's to compare Madison to other state public schools.

Guidelines Used for Each Grade

Throughout this study, guidelines were used to compare the expectations of teachers for student achievement with those in other school systems, particularly the Palo Alto Unified School District in California. Palo Alto Unified was chosen primarily because of the clear, precise learning objectives for each grade and the author's belief that average children, urban or rural, rich or poor, are capable of reaching the learning objectives cited. Not all learning objectives were included for each grade, because some relied upon audiovisual or computer technology in the classroom, which was not available in Madison. In addition, the California framework for subjects (K–12) was used to arrive at a general overall scope of learning objectives for each grade in each subject.

The average student should master basic reading and math skills in the first four grades. Processing of information from kindergarten through the fourth grade is the foundation of critical thinking. This maturation process occurs not only horizontally but vertically by integrating concrete horizontal reading and math materials into a vertical creative abstraction of ideas and a world view. The scores shown in table 7.1 are only a barometer, not a total assessment. They are lower than the state norms in kindergarten and about at par in the fourth grade. Sometimes a systemic sporadic performance is the result of too large a class load, or having to cope with outmoded textbooks. But this system had a one to fifteen ratio with a teacher aide for most of the day. The standard Houghton Mifflin texts were used for each grade. What the scores do indicate is an uneven performance, the reasons for which were found in the classroom evaluation: learning environment, teaching methodology, and teacher prognostication of student capability.

The evaluation was conducted over six months. All classrooms were visited, some several times during that six months. Each classroom visit lasted several hours to give the students and teachers time to get used to having the evaluator in the classroom.

Learning Environment

Learning environment reflects individual teacher creativity, the effort used to reinforce learning and engage students in their own learning process, and the comfort zone of a safe, as opposed to judgmental, atmosphere. Posters, student displays, visual symbols of role models, maps, reading books on shelves, special sections within the room for extracurricular learning, such as games and art centers, all play significant roles in making a classroom an interesting place.

The singular feature throughout the Madison system is, without exception, the lack of anything remotely connected with Indian culture on the walls. This visual vacuum indicates to the 70 percent Indian student population that they do not exist. Even the bookshelves are devoid of any Indian subject matter.

At the time of the study, the classrooms were too large for the number of students. This allowed students to spread out and made it more difficult for teachers to maintain eye contact with each student. The ceilings were unusually high, and teachers tended to place posters high up along the wall. In the kindergarten class, for instance, picture displays were edged along the ceiling, which means someone used a ladder to put them up. Common sense says that if you want children to learn from these displays, they should be at a child's eye level. In the first-, second-, and third-grade classrooms, posters, and samples of the children's work were better placed. A new third-grade teacher's classroom reflected her interest in science: there were paper skeletons around the class walls, each labeled with a student's name along with parts of the body.

One fourth-grade class had maps edging the ten-foot ceilings, and the room was intentionally kept very dark. In contrast, another fourth-grade teacher filled the room with visually stimulating maps, posters, and drawings at eye level. Some classrooms were sectioned off with tables of books, games, and learning centers, which reduced the unusually large spaces into a more comfortable setting. For the most part, teachers kept to the rigid traditional form of seats in rows front to back, with the teacher's desk in the front.

Teaching Methodology

As teachers mature, they develop a style that they find comfortable and expedient. New teachers bring fresh thinking to the classroom, but they have not had time to develop organization. Older teachers are better organized, but, sometimes lack spontaneity. This system had the extremes of neophytes in their first year of teaching and highly experienced teachers who had been in the system at least ten years.

The kindergarten teacher was in her first year of teaching. She was responsible for three sections of two hours each. She was left to sink or swim on her own. We observed a story time. The book she had chosen was not connected to the rural multicultural mix in her classroom and the children seemed uninterested. The teacher shifted gears by putting on a record and having the students dance in a circle to the song. One Indian fledgling was adamant in remaining seated. The teacher prodded the child to enter into the circle, but every time there was a break in the music, the child sat down at her desk. Within fifteen minutes, the teacher was exhausted trying to deal with the child. Finally, the Indian teacher aide who evidently knew the child spoke to her, and the child joined in once again.

The classroom lesson was on "D" sounds. Some of the children joined in, but most did not. The ones who did not respond were predominantly the Indian children. The teacher had eye contact with the children, predominantly white, who were responding to her.

Some teachers go to summer school to upgrade their skills. An example of how rewarding that experience can be was the first grade teacher, who learned a new method of teaching sums. The math speed and accuracy of her students was truly remarkable. They enjoyed the challenges she presented to them. By contrast, the other first-grade teacher taught sums by rote. Her students were apathetic.

The second-grade teachers used the Houghton Mifflin series exclusively, and felt their students were not reading as well as they should. They believed the contributing factors were insufficient high-interest books in the classroom and the elimination of an art teacher through budget cuts. When pressed, they reported that art lessons improved self-esteem and made it easier for students to learn to read.

The two third-grade teachers also used the Houghton Mifflin series. The experienced teacher encouraged dialogue by using the question segments at the end of each chapter. To teach her science class, she had students grow molds and seeds. She was wary of a computer as a learning tool in the classroom and questioned the wisdom of eliminating the position of school nurse to whom she had been able to send students for physical and emotional problems. She questioned whether the discipline policy with heavy emphasis on suspension was really wise. She was critical of the fact that the school did not have a good art program because she also felt that this subject was important to improve self-esteem.

The other third-grade teacher was in her second year. Her fresh approach and creative interest in science were immediately evident. She made her own science work sheets because she viewed her science texts as outmoded. She moved around the classroom and held student interest. She wanted a computer in the classroom. She had not used the question segments at the end of each chapter in the Mifflin series and admitted that her inexperience made it difficult to teach students with disparate abilities. She had not thought about developing individual education plans to bring her students up to parity. In fact, she did not know what they were.[2] She appeared to have good command of her class, and there was every indication that she would be an excellent teacher given time and experience.

One fourth-grade teacher was unexperienced, and the other was a twenty-year veteran. The neophyte organized his classroom in ways that minimized eye contact with the students. During the time of on-site evaluation he did not leave his chair to maintain control of students in the back of the classroom. He also missed opportunities to interact with students because of his traditional seating arrangement. In fact, during the site visit, a student had his hand raised to ask a question a full five minutes before the teacher saw him. The teacher reported difficulty maintaining control in the classroom.

Even though he minimized student-teacher interaction, this teacher's willingness to work with individual students at his desk was evident. He had been trained for and used IEPs. He enjoyed teaching, but his ambitions lay in the completion of his master's degree program so that he would qualify for an administrative position. He wanted a computer in the classroom because he thought it would increase retention, particularly in English and math.

The other fourth-grade teacher circulated around the classroom and maintained eye contact with all the students. Her one bad habit was impatience with student response. She asked a question, and when the response was not quick enough, she answered the question herself. Worse yet, she sometimes did not explain her answer, but went quickly on to the next question. She felt the primary system needed an art teacher, a multipurpose room, and computers in the classrooms. She thought she could do more science experiments if her room had a sink in it. She was pessimistic about any changes in the system because requests were ignored by the administration. She reported difficulty in communicating with some parents.

By the end of the first round of classroom visits, there appeared to be a teaching pattern that needed substantiation through empirical data. A mapped-out grid was arranged in the same pattern as each classroom, with name and race of the children drawn into each square. Every question, response, and eye contact was noted within the grid. The result showed that Indian students predominantly occupied seats to the left or the right of the center and toward the back, in contrast to the white students who were seated in the center and toward the front in all grades. Teacher stations were front and center. This grid provided evidence that Indian students received less attention, time, and eye contact than white students.

Experienced teachers circled around the class, forcing students to visually connect with them. Nonetheless, during classroom discussions, it was evident that most teachers were uncomfortable with silence. They did not give students sufficient time to digest the questions being asked and frame a response. Indian children are socialized to reflect before speaking. Non-Indian children were decidedly quicker and more responsive. Teachers misinterpreted the delayed responses of Indian students, which is compelling evidence that, experience notwithstanding, they had not acquired understanding of culturally different learning styles.

The discovery method was used by a number of teachers in this system. However, when faced with losing control, they invariably resorted to rote learning, which had the unforeseen effect of increasing, rather than decreasing, student hyperactivity. Maintaining control is reported to be a major concern in this system. The methods used varied from using the extreme of a system-wide suspension policy for major and (some complain) minor infractions of the rules, to one third-grade teacher who placed an Indian student's desk in a corner near the door, separated from the rest of the student body. She informed me that she did no know why, but this student found it impossible to concentrate unless removed from all other students. She assured me that she had the parent's consent for this move. She reported the child was being seen by a counselor.

Learning Objectives

Kindergarten children are mature enough to listen to stories, dramatizations, and poetry; understand and share experiences; dictate original stories; supply rhymes to a given work; recall and repeat a story, song, or poem from memory.

They can recognize their names in print, and they can name letters, match capital and small letters, copy letters, develop left to right and front to back order of a book. They can recall story events in sequence and remember character names, main ideas, and conclusion of stories. They can write their names, know correct letter formation for most letters, and know that sentences begin with capital letters, and recognize simple punctuation.

Even at this early age, they are capable of mastering math concepts, including number values one through ten; the vocabulary of comparison, size, position, time, weight, and so on; and symbolic representation from concrete to abstract and vice-versa, that is, graphs. They can count, recognize simple geometric shapes, such as circle, square, triangle, rectangle; use positional and area terms, such as inside, outside, whole, one-half; recognize symmetry; and add and subtract using manipulative materials. They can develop an awareness of self, friendship, and family roles and know varieties of families in their environment.

Science should be started in kindergarten and can include exploration of the processes of science, such as observing, comparing, and classifying, hypothesizing, predicting, and collecting data; studying natural and physical phenomena in child's environment, such as plants, animals, rocks, sands, water, heat, and magnetism, as may be appropriate; awareness of time sequence, such as seasons, day, night, and the calendar.

Appropriate music and art skills for kindergarten children include expression through movement and singing; learning to sing a variety of songs, such as folk, traditional and seasonal; body movements, dance awareness of color, texture, form, space, size, line; use of a variety of media, such as paint, clay, and crayon; increased skills in artistic expression, such as cutting, drawing, painting, and construction; and awareness of differences in styles of art.

The kindergarten teacher had very modest expectations of intellectual development for her students. She did not consider her students sufficiently mature to accomplish more than sitting and listening to stories, learning the alphabet in upper and lower case, and learning basic numbers. However, she only had each class for two hours a day, which may account for the chasm between the expectations and the potential of the teacher for this grade.

Reading

First graders can master word-multiple meanings of words, some antonyms and synonyms and recognize the sound symbol corresponding to consonants. They can learn single consonant sounds in initial, middle, and final positions: short and long vowel sounds; most consonant blends; some compound words and word endings; the contractions; and common word families.

Comprehension

An average first grader can understand that printed symbols represent objects or actions; follow printed directions; draw conclusions from given facts; recall what has been read aloud; place events in sequence; remember where to find answers to questions; tell main story ideas; recall details; recognize a statement as an answer to a question; distinguish between fact and fantasy; predict outcomes; and classify objects. They are also capable of writing words, phrases, titles for pictures, complete sentences. They are capable of participating in group discussion.

The first-grade teachers listed the acquisition of phonetic rules, beginning consonants, spelling and grammar skills, addition and subtraction of numbers from one to ten being able to tell time, money, half fractions, and measuring as minimal goals. Being able to read simple books was an optimum goal. These modest expectations overlook half of the English and language arts program listed below, the contents of which place substantial emphasis on the introduction of reasoning, abstraction, and analysis.

Second graders should be able to write stories and poems, master punctuation, use reference materials, analyze stories, reflect on what is being read, distinguish between fact and fantasy, and begin to write cursive. In social studies, a second grader should be able to define map symbols, locate directions, and recognize land forms and water bodies. In science, a second grader can investigate nature and report on it and begin interpreting data and drawing up small experiments.

Second-grade teachers identified minimal educational objectives as reading, writing long paragraphs and stories about animals, using compound words, vocabulary, addition, subtraction, multiplication, and division. Responses were vague, lacking articulation of optimal skills for this grade. When directly asked whether a second grader was sufficiently mature to research and write a paper on an assigned topic, they replied in the negative.

Third graders should be able to supply common synonyms, antonyms, and homonyms; identify root words; know prefixes, contractions, and suffixes; comprehend stories; predict outcomes of a story; understand different literary forms; master techniques of skimming and summarizing; and learn to use dictionaries, encyclopedias, indexes, glossaries, charts, graphs, and diagrams.

They should be able to read fluently and out loud; listen in a group; report observations, facts and ideas, tell a story; write poetry and simple reports; and analyze paragraphs. They can spell frequently used words; know proper grammar; recognize the difference between a noun and a pronoun; recognize tenses; use proper punctuation and capitalization; write neatly in upper- and lowercase cursive letters.

In mathematics, third graders can master addition and subtraction of two- and three-digit numbers with and without regrouping, know and use multiplication and division facts, add and subtract amounts of money written in standard dollar notation.

Third graders can tell time; determine and distinguish appropriate units of measurements, such as inch, foot, yard or mile; find the area of a rectangle by counting squares and volume by counting cubes; identify the fraction of a whole and the fractional part of a set of objects; and compare numbers using symbols.

Third graders can master the concept of a globe; identify major bodies of water, continents, countries, and cities; locate places on the globe in terms of four main directions; locate the equator and Arctic/Antarctic circles. They can analyze the importance of lakes and waterways and how the environment affects their daily life and develop a global perspective beginning with their area and how that area is linked to the state, the nation, and the rest of the world.

Third-grade science should include exploration and investigation of natural science, physical science, and earth/space science; understand and experience observation, classification, inferential, and experimental processes; text hypothesis; collecting, organizing, and interpreting data; predicting, measuring, and identifying controlling variables.

Third-grade art should include examination of color, lines, shapes, textures, and forms; drawing; painting; printing; modeling; constructing; and beginning knowledge of famous artists.

Third-grade teachers identified minimal objectives as being able to read, use of compound words, increased vocabulary skills, writing long paragraphs and stories about animals, the acquisition of addition, subtraction, multiplication, division, fractions, and basic geometry. With the exception of fractions and basic geometry, third-grade teachers viewed their objectives as the same as those of the second grade.

Whatever the deficiencies of the first educational milestone, the strength of the fourth-grade faculty appears to have closed the gap, and, in fact, in some instances, surpassed the state norms.

An average fourth-grade student learns new words and uses them within context, recognizes plurals and hyphenated words, gets the meanings of words from context, and can identify figurative language. Word attack skills include a review of consonant blends, mastery of prefixes and suffixes, and the ability to decode multisyllabic words. They should be able to read a story, find the main idea, identify details, generalize, predict outcomes, use context clues, take notes, and outline. They should master the reading of poetry, be exposed to good literature, and read silently for a sustained period.

Fourth-grade teachers identified instructional goals as bringing students up to their age-grade level, writing one or two stories a week, science experiments which inculcate a greater understanding of the universe and its ecosystem, and a minimum grade of 80 percent or better in math tests.

Summary of Grades K through 4

Half of the teachers of kindergarten through fourth grade were nontenured because there is a high turnover rate in this school. Consequently, there was a wide range of teaching experience and competence in all grades. All were certified for the grades they taught.

Teachers used the same Houghton Mifflin series but were left to fend for themselves in the ways this series was used. They were ill at ease about defining skills their students should master before the end of the year. There was a significant gap between what the teachers thought children in their grade could learn and the guidelines listed. Placing maps and visual aids out of the eye level of young children was counterproductive to learning. There appeared to be little structure, supervision, or communication between faculty and administration.

Teaching methodology tended to concentrate on the more verbal, non-Indian students, depriving the Indian students of equality in education. There are studies addressing the "cross-over" effect in Indian education. This occurs when Indian children internalize racial differences and associate these differences as negative. By consistently acknowledging the more verbal non-Indian student, teachers inadvertently sent negative messages to students about racial differences and eroded the Indian student's self-esteem. In addition, classrooms lacked any posters, art work, literature, representing a positive role models of their race.

Stacks of Indian education materials, including books, worksheets, audio-visual and computer programs were available to any teacher who visited either the reservation, the tribal education department, or the Title 4 Indian education mobile office attached to the Madison school. No teacher used any of these resources.

Two hours a day were allocated for each kindergarten class. In a survey conducted after the on-site observations, the question was asked whether two hours was sufficient for this grade. Ninety-five percent of the teachers thought the kindergarten program adequate. The principal thought it to be inadequate but lacked sufficient leadership to set higher standards even though the inexperienced kindergarten teachers would probably have welcomed some guidelines.

8

The Gap Widens: Grades Five through Eight

Fifth and Sixth Grades

Ask an adult the name of his or her fifth-grade teachers. Very likely will remember not only the name(s) but offer a description and relate some classroom experience during that year. Some recall other teachers, but almost all will remember who taught them in the fifth grade.[1] Piaget defined this as the maturation stage when the ability to discern abstract from concrete knowledge is crystallized.

The mastery of basic reading, math, and comprehension skills should be behind a fifth grader. Ahead is a global world of ideas. This maturation process, which appears to come on so suddenly, is like a new toy for a fifth grader. This is the delightful stage when light bulbs go off in the mind, when they practice mental dexterity with as much joy as a sport, and when the process of critical thinking crystallizes as they link one abstract idea with a distant other.

This developmental stage is so profound that a teacher conveying positive self-images to students will have a classroom filled with students make every effort to please. The Pygmalion effect is never so crystal clear as at this grade level.

The fifth-grade Madison scores were about at par with state levels, except for reading and reference materials (see table 8.1). This subject may seem inconsequential, but with these skills a student can find out information on any subject; without them they must accept either what information is readily available or narrow their curiosity to interests within the classroom framework. Around the fifth grade, Indian students experience the cross-over effect,

Table 8.1   SRA Scores for Grades 5 through 8

	FIFTH GRADE	
	Madison	State
Reading	6.5	7.2
Mathematics	6.9	6.7
Language Arts	7.5	7.4
Reference Materials	8.2	7.5
Social Studies	7.4	7.6
Science	7.7	7.7
	SIXTH GRADE	
	Madison	State
Reading	7.9	8.4
Mathematics	7.2	8.3
Language Arts	8.5	8.3
Reference Materials	8.7	9.0
Social Studies	7.8	8.6
Science	9.0	8.9
	SEVENTH GRADE	
	Madison	State
Reading	8.5	9.6
Mathematics	7.4	9.4
Language Arts	7.8	9.2
Reference Materials	6.9	10.0
Social Studies	7.9	9.9
Science	7.8	10.0
	EIGHTH GRADE	
	Madison	State
Reading	9.8	10.2
Mathematics	8.8	11.7
Language Arts	9.4	10.8
Reference Materials	9.6	10.7
Social Studies	9.7	10.9
Science	9.8	11.2

which has a profound influence on academic achievement. They become aware and internalize race and racism.

In contrast to the fifth grader, the sixth grader is an educational challenge. The intellectually wide-eyed fifth grader generates a mouthy, robust, and somewhat moody sixth grader. Sixth graders are at a stage when they begin to want and need more autonomy in their lives. Except for science and language arts, sixth-grade Madison students were behind the state age-grade norm. The gap was most significant in mathematics, where the students scored better than the state norms in the fifth grade, but were a year behind in the sixth grade.

Teaching the sixth grade requires a balancing act between providing the essential structure for learning, while at the same time encouraging autonomy. Contemporary teaching theory suggests using individual education plans to instill structure and autonomy, but the Madison teachers were not comfortable or well-trained in this method.

Teachers in the Madison system have both grades in the same classroom at the same time. During the classroom observations it became evident that the teachers were using the same methodology for both grades, either giving the fifth graders more autonomy than they could absorb or giving more structure than was necessary or desirable for the sixth graders. This led to classroom management problems, which was a contributing factor in the academic achievement of the sixth grade.

Reading

Learning Objectives Fifth-Sixth Grade. Students in these grades should be reading a wide range of fiction, nonfiction, and newspapers. They should be able to explore poetry, myths, and biographies, and they should be introduced to new ideas. They should be able to discuss and analyze characters and plots of the books they read. The goal expressed by the teacher of this class was to inculcate a love for reading, but books chosen for her classes lacked the sophistication which would interest this age-grade. The books appeared to be largely picture books, and while this may be largely a visual society—even adults often choose newspapers and magazines for their visual content—it is important to introduce and expose children to an imaginative world of ideas. Tried and true books by authors such as C. S. Lewis's, Jack London, Joy Adamson, and Frances Hodgson are normal reading fare for this age, as well as biographies of sports heroes, famous people such as Helen Keller, or science fiction, none of which were in this classroom. The class was not reading at par with state levels, partly because the teacher's expectations of what students were capable of reading at this age was below their maturation level. She expressed apprehension about installing a computer in her classroom and was critical of the Madison administration's dismissal of a school nurse and art teacher.

Teaching Methodology. The fifth-sixth grade reading teacher had twenty-two years of experience and additional training beyond her initial certification B.A. She used the Houghton Mifflin series and relied exclusively on the text to stimulate dialogue. The fifth-grade SRA scores were seven months behind and the sixth-grade were five months behind. When queried about using individual education plans the teacher responded that she liked the concept but did not have experience or training in developing an IEP. She thought the problem with her classroom was the wide range of reading capability of the students.

Learning Environment. The classroom of the fifth-sixth grade reading teacher displayed a few posters, none representing Indians. The bookshelves lining the walls were devoid of Indian authors, biographies, or histories, nor did she know of any Indian writers.

Language Arts

Learning Objectives. A modest learning expectation of the fifth grade student should be to summarize; take notes; identify ideas of a paragraph; and know how to outline, edit, improve *from suggestions,* expand notes to prose, rewrite a story or article, and write reports and business and social letters. Students should acquire oral skills for group participation discussions and elaborate and describe details. A sixth grader should be able to write stories, poems, and reports and summarize, edit, rewrite, and describe with detail anything that is read and discussed orally. Both these grades should master every aspect of punctuation, grammar, and spelling. The SRA scores indicate that the Madison students are on par with the state norms in language arts. This is surprising because the teacher expressed his maximum expectation for these students as being able to write cursive and print, give a complete thought, spell most words, use the dictionary, and be articulate. The fifth-sixth grade language arts teacher had taught for eight years, but this was his first year at the Madison school. He planned on going into administration, and was working to complete his master's program to achieve that goal.

Learning Environment. Classroom was devoid of visual aids, student works, or posters. The overall impression was stark, unimaginative, and cold.

Teaching Methodology. This teacher's priority was creative writing, and he required three written essays a week in the beginning of the term. He responded vaguely when asked about the length of the papers to be written, the number of books to be read monthly, or requirements for research papers. He did not respond when asked what standards he used in marking the papers. He did not require much reading in his class, because he relied on the reading teacher for that instructional function. He expressed the need for a better phonic system, as well as a spelling program. He wanted a computer in the classroom.

Social Studies

Learning Objectives. The focus of fifth-grade social studies is an understanding of the United States. A reasonable learning expectation for this grade is a mastery of geography vocabulary; understanding different versions of maps, legends, scales symbols, and their uses; identifying natural and political boundaries; and identifying major cities and states. They should acquire an understanding of the complex culture of American Indians before the arrival of Europeans and the foundation of the American political system, and they should be able to extrapolate from that knowledge the concept of the connection the United States has to the rest of the world.

Students should be able to use map skills; understand and correlate longitude with latitude so that they can locate any place on earth; identify continents, oceans, and major countries of the world; and understand time zones, meridian, and international date lines.

Sixth graders should be able to understand alternate perspectives, interdependence of nations in world trade, social issues, and the impact of culture on different peoples of the world.

Teaching Objectives. The fifth-sixth-grade social studies teacher expressed her goals for the fifth grade minimally was for them to know the fifty states, know the basis of government in the United States, how to read a map, keys and direction finders on maps, and to be able to write and read reports and use reference materials.

The sixth-grade emphasized world perspectives. She expected students to know the seven continents, understand countries and the religions of the world, have a basic knowledge of the middle ages, and develop research and public speaking skills.

Learning Environment. The social studies teacher was in her third year of teaching. She had done extensive traveling and conveyed her joy of learning about different places and people to her students. Her classroom walls were covered with maps and brochures from different countries. She set her classroom up in small learning modules, so that four or five students work together. She had less than fifteen fifth-sixth graders in the same room at the same time. She wanted a computer in the classroom and thought this would increase her teaching effectiveness.

Teaching Methodology. This teacher moved around the classroom and spent time with each module. She had a great deal of enthusiasm for teaching this subject. She prepared learning units about American Indians from materials she had acquired from the education center on the reservation and had also prepared units on African Americans and women for her students. Her students attain an average in fifth-grade social studies which is almost at the norm for the state. In the sixth grade her class averaged below the state norms. It is likely that she was teaching both grades at the same levels and had difficulty separating instructional goals for the sixth graders.

Math

Aside from reading and language art skills, the single most significant subject that determines future career choices is math. This subject provides a foundation for science, engineering, and health-related fields.[2] Comparing the state with the Madison SRA scores offers concrete evidence that students will be severely handicapped if they choose to enter math-oriented careers, unless they enter remedial programs to bring them up to par in high school (see table 8.2).

Learning Objectives. Fifth graders should be able to master numerals of nine or fewer digits, find sums of two or more whole numbers with or without grouping, read and write decimals through thousandths, use multiplication and division algorithms, use estimates to find products or quotients, find the common and lowest term factor, find the least common denominator, subtract fractions with unlike denominators, and find equal ratios using ratio tables.

It is not overly ambitious for fifth graders to master elementary geometry; find length, radius, diameter, area of a rectangle or triangle, find perimeter and volume of a rectangle; estimate capacity and weight; change an expression of a measurement from one unit to an expression with a larger/smaller unit; identify parallel and perpendicular lines right or obtuse, or acute angles; count the faces, edges, and vertices of a space figure; give the coordinates of points and graphs points in the coordinate plane.

Sixth graders should be able to read and write standard numerals: round whole numbers or decimals; add, subtract, multiply, and divide whole numbers and decimals; master fractions, percentage, and integers.

In geometry, sixth graders should be able to use traditional and metric units of measure in finding length, capacity, weight, temperature, area and volume: find the areas of rectangles, triangles, and circles, by using the formulas, find the volume of a box by using a formula, measure angles; construct congruent segments, angles, and triangles; identify parallel, perpendicular, and skew

Table 8.2 SRA Math Scores

Grade	Madison	State
1	1.7	2.3
2	3.0	3.5
3	3.9	4.6
4	5.5	5.6
5	6.9	6.7
6	7.2	8.3
7	7.4	9.4
8	8.8	11.7

lines; count faces, edges, and vertices of a space figure; relate points and coordinates; apply mathematics in relevant problem-solving situations; use problem-solving skills involving unit changes within the metric system and the traditional system; read, interpret, and construct graphs; and find the probability of an outcome.

The math teacher had difficulty communicating to the students, even though his love for the subject was evident. Math is difficult to communicate to students, and he was perplexed by their inability to understand what appeared to be elemental to him. His almost monosyllabic response to the students' questions was consistent with his response to my questions. When asked to identify minimum math mastery for each grade, he responded by opening up the text and referring to it.

Teaching Methodology. The math teacher was new to teaching and to Madison. His text was the standard Houghton Mifflin series. He used rote learning methods and the blackboard extensively, rarely moving around the class to see if the students understood solutions. He also taught down to the sixth grade.

Learning Environment. The math teacher's voice and body language did not convey the excitement he had for the subject. His classroom was set up raditionally and was barren of math charts or visual aids.

Science

The science teacher was tenured and had been teaching for a decade. This system does not have a science laboratory and cannot afford field trips to a science museum within the state. It has no organized science club nor have they participated in state or regional science fairs. This teacher overcame some of these handicaps because her students were at par with state fifth-sixth grade levels. She used the standard Houghton Mifflin series.

Seventh and Eighth Grades

The linear correlation between grade, norms, and teacher is more diffused from the seventh grade onward in the Madison system. The same teacher might be assigned different grades in one subject, or several teachers might be responsible for different sections in one subject. From the seventh grade on, evaluations of teaching and classroom environment were done by department rather than by an individual teacher.

Reading and Language Arts

The head of the English Department at Madison submitted an outline of the grade-by-grade systematic program in reading and language arts subheaded for comprehension, study skills, vocabulary, research skills, oral reading skills, discussion techniques, and reading rates. This was admirable except for the fact that when interviewed, none of the teachers reported that they had seen this plan. The plan had an additional flaw. The guidelines left out specifics. Although it is a worthwhile objective to increase a child's vocabulary, or have that child read classics, specific vocabulary and classics were not given. Two of the teachers felt that the seventh grade was a transitional year. Consequently more time was spent in easing students into becoming more self-directed mentally and emotionally than in academics. They also felt that there was a serious problem in discipline. All teachers had the spatial problems of large classrooms and few students, allowing students to spread out and making it difficult to maintain contact. There was evidence of teacher dedication in the classroom visitations, but in spite of this, and probably because teachers were left in a vacuum without guidance, the evidence of SRA standings suggests this department expected very little of its students. The department placed academic goals for these grades as the acquisition of spelling and grammar, writing reports, and a minimum of creative expression. There was no student newspaper or drama club.

Over-all, the English department had the most experienced teachers, which should have been reflected in the classroom environment. However, one English teacher decorated her classroom with teddy bears, hardly appropriate for the age of her students. Another was conducting a course titled "Positive Images," the focus of which was communication, body language, and self-esteem. Her classroom had a poster on the wall which read:

Richard Cory

So on we worked and waited for the light
and went without the meat and cursed the bread
and Richard Cory one calm summer night
went home and put a bullet through his head

Very little if any thought was given to the classroom environment even though the department had sound, experienced teachers who encouraged, even demanded, dialogue with students. A class in Shakespeare provided stimulating student interaction and discussions about character and plots, as did a class in self-esteem and body language. Yet, the disparity between the school and state norms was too significant to be overlooked (see table 8.1).

Learning Objectives. An exemplary seventh- and eighth-grade reading/language arts program should place emphasis on the development of creativity and a wide variety of writing experiences. This includes short narratives; story openings and endings; imaginary cast of characters for plays and stories; descriptions; both subjectives and objectives of people, places, objects, and events. The skills that should be developed are writing and evaluating each other's papers and use of vivid imagery, including metaphors, similes, and appeals to senses. Specific exercises in class should emphasize image making with guided daydreams, word games, illustrating words, writing to music, and observation of photographs and imagining what happened before and after the action depicted.

In the eighth grade, students are sufficiently mature and should have acquired the skills to publish a literary magazine, newspaper, or yearbook. In that vein, they should be able to understand and develop skills in layout and design, photography, interviewing, writing, editing, and advertising.

Seventh and eighth graders should acquire a solid foundation in the classics, biographies, autobiographies, science fiction, fantasy, legend, and myth, fables, short stores, transcripts, plays, poetry, memoirs, diaries, letters, articles, and eyewitness reporting.

Mathematics

Virtually any profession in the sciences, engineering, and medicine is closed to students who have not mastered mathematics. The Madison math teachers appeared to have great difficulty in classroom management. In fact, complaints were made by parents of the teachers being too abrupt and combative with the students. During classroom observations, these complaints were confirmed.

By the end of eighth grade, students should have acquired knowledge of math, algebra, and basic trigonometry. Since Madison is behind the state norms by three years at the end of the eighth grade, it is evident that math instruction is below par.

Science

Learning Objectives. Courses should extensively cover astronomy, oceanography, geology, meteorology, and botany. Students at this stage of development generally like science. The Madison science department was without a laboratory, and the textbooks were outdated (eight years old). The Science Department faculty lacked enthusiasm, possibly because they were without the basic tools with which to teach science intelligently and creatively. Apathy was evident in the classroom as the demeanor of students and teacher was very subdued. Almost certainly, the absence of a laboratory for some hands-on experiments contributed to lowering both teacher and student enthusiasm for science. Table 8.1 shows the gap between the Madison system and the state norm, due in large part to the lack of a science laboratory.

Social Studies

The social-studies program had some of the most experienced teachers in the system. The students left sixth grade with a 7.8 norm in social studies. In the seventh grade they advanced by only one month. Although they were behind one year and two months from the state norms, they managed to accelerate their progress two years by the end of the eighth grade. Apparently, their strength was in teaching the eighth grade.

The students do not take SRAs in the twelfth grade. They do take ACT tests measuring a composite score in English, math, social studies, and natural science.

The senior high school teachers had the most experience, longevity, and influence in the system. Paradoxically, they were also the system's weakest academic link. They had begun teaching at Madison when the student body was exclusively white. They expressed a correlation between the new Indian student body and declining academic performance. They asserted that drugs and alcohol were responsible for student apathy and/or aggressiveness, that (Indian) parents did not care about the education of their children, and that the students themselves did not apply themselves to learning. On a positive note, dropouts from Madison were almost nonexistent. However, the school graduated students far below the level necessary for successful entry into college. This was not a handicap until recently, when the open enrollment state university system developed new, more rigorous, high-school requirements for college entry.

The senior high faculty devised a discipline policy for the Madison system, which placed heavy emphasis on suspension. Even though few classes have more than fifteen students (most have ten or fewer), they felt those students who were "troublemakers" should be suspended.

The apathy expressed by senior faculty was contagious. Newer teachers with fresh ideas were told that everything had been tried already to improve the situation. In the past decade, two Indians were hired, but they left after their first year. It is reported that the changes suggested by these Indian teachers were discouraged by the senior faculty, and they were left either with accepting the status quo, or with resigning. Interviews with current new faculty say that they knew about the instructional guidelines, but have not seen them, and those who have seen them say they are useless unless everyone follows them. Academic leadership was provided by a senior teacher who was also the mayor of Madison and married to the head of the English Department. As mayor, he had not supported an increase in taxes to provide for a science laboratory, newer texts, library books, or an art studio. The school library provides concrete evidence of the minimal effort being made to support education.

Senior High School

Classroom Environment

Few of the classrooms had pictures or posters of any kind, and none had pictures, posters, or books representing Indian people or culture. The hallways were plastered with posters about drinking and driving and drugs, symbols representing negative behavior.

Teaching Methodology

All of the classrooms in the high school were set up traditionally, with the teacher station in front and student desks in five or six rows. The rooms were oversized for the few students in each class, so students spread out all over the rooms, most sitting as far away from the teacher as possible. Teachers consistently used the rote method. Even though classes were small, the interaction between students and teachers was minimal, and this alienation of teacher and student was visible. Indian culture was included in the instructional guidelines for most subjects, but no one reported these had ever been implemented.

One of the cherished myths about Indians is that they are excellent athletes. Apparently there were a high number of "accidents" occurring in the Physical Education and sports program activities. The sports coach valued competition and pushed students beyond normal physical abilities. According to Indian parents, the physical education program can be hazardous to children's health.

The art program was directed by a former artist, a maverick who appeared to have good rapport with the students. It is hard to say whether his classes were being taught well because the facility was so small and cramped and the supplies limited. The artwork the students displayed throughout the class was impressive, and one can only speculate what kind of work these students could do with a proper art studio.

The vocational-technical education facility was separate from the main school. It consisted of an old car and some engine parts in a large, barn-like building. The students were mostly mulling around without supervision. This program came under fire from the regional accreditation authorities.

Summary

At the end of the ninth grade, students averaged 10.9 in reading, which was better than the state average. By the end of the eleventh grade, students averaged 11.1, which means that in three years they had increased their skills only by two months (see table 8.3).

At the end of the ninth grade, students averaged 11.2 in language arts, which was better than the state average. By the end of the eleventh grade, students averaged 11.6, which means that in three years they had increased their skills only by four months.

At the end of the ninth grade, students averaged 10.4 in reference materials, which was lower than the state norms by four months. By the end of the eleventh grade, students averaged 11.0., which means that in three years they had increased their skills only by six months.

At the end of the ninth grade, students averaged 10.0 in mathematics, which was two years and 7 months below the state norm. By the end of the eleventh grade, students averaged 12.7, which was exactly at par with the state norms.

Table 8.3 SRA Scores for Grades 9 through 11

	NINTH GRADE	
	Madison	State
Reading	10.9	10.8
Language Arts	11.2	11.1
Reference Materials	10.4	10.8
Mathematics	10.0	12.7
Social Studies	10.4	10.6
Science	10.6	11.8
	TENTH GRADE	
Reading	11.1	11.8
Science	10.6	11.8
Mathematics	12.7	12.7
Language Arts	12.1	12.0
Reference Materials	12.0	11.9
Social Studies	10.6	11.9
	ELEVENTH GRADE	
Reading	11.6	12.7
Mathematics	12.7	12.7
Language Arts	11.6	12.7
Reference Materials	11.0	12.7
Social Studies	11.0	12.7
Science	11.1	12.7

By the end of the ninth grade, students averaged 10.4 in social studies, which was two months behind the state norm. By the end of the eleventh grade, students averaged 11.0, which means they had only increased their skills only by six months in three years.

By the end of the ninth grade, students averaged 10.6 in science, one year and two months behind the state norm. By the end of the eleventh grade, students averaged 11.1, which means they had increased their skills only by seven months in three years.

The composite twelfth-grade scores of Madison students ranked in the fifty-sixth percentile.

The senior faculty had ignored and/or demeaned multicultural education. In so doing, they had contributed undermining educational achievement for all students in the system. In 1985, thirty students graduated from Madison with an average GPA of 2.37. In 1986, thirty-one students graduated with an average GPA of 2.60. In 1987, thirty students attained an average GPA of 2.57 (see table

8.4). In plain words, Madison's graduates barely qualified for entry into a university, nursing school, business training, or any other posthigh-school program. Even if they qualified for higher education by virtue of their GPAs, the average Madison student was still more than a year and a half behind in most subjects they would encounter in their freshman year. Some students will make it through college through sheer determination and hard work. Most will dropout or be disqualified in their freshman year. And the cycle continues.

The School Libraries

Grade School

With the exception of teacher who used the facility to teach chess to his students, there was very little use made of the grammar-school library. The library was located in a hall outside of the kindergarten through third grade classroom. Teachers asserted that books were checked out during class time, but this was not evident. There was no librarian, and the stacks did not look as if they were used very often, some having a good deal of dust. The library closed as soon as class was over. Of the grammar and high school collection, 120 books were selected at random for a fourteen-hour review. Grammar-school books were dirty and dilapidated, and pages were missing from many of them. Most of them had been published between 1930 and 1970. The explosion in children's books that took place during the seventies and eighties has not touched the Madison library.

Many of the books about American Indians were derogatory, demeaning, and contained negative stereotypes. There was scant evidence of books about other minorities or women and there was little information on other world cultures or nations.

Table 8.4 Average Composite Score of Madison (in Percentile)

1982	56.25
1983	32.17
1984	40.1
1985	51.47
1986	56.84

High School

The high-school library had come under heavy criticism by the accreditation team who found the collection inadequate. It was reported that the deficiency was rectified. However, this was misleading, because the number of books may have been increased to a standard level, but the quality still left a good deal to be desired. In the reference section, there were approximately nineteen different sets of specialized-subject encyclopedias. Three sets were printed in 1957, five sets were printed from 1961 to 1969, seven sets were printed from 1973 to 1979, and four sets were printed since 1982.

It was reported that there were four thousand books in the library, although that was unlikely. One of the survey questions concerned how the faculty and principals perceived the adequacy of the school library. The results are shown in figure 8.1 below.

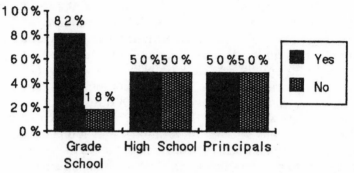

Figure 8.1   Our School Library Is Adequate to Meet Student Needs

Half of the high-school and 82 percent of the grade-school faculty do not perceive the school library as substandard.

9

The Survey

Indian students typically attend rural public schools located near or adjacent to their reservations. It is not surprising that the rural Madison study echoes urban Indian education studies, meaning the findings in this study can be generalized to conditions Indian students encounter in the nation's public school systems. The factors contributing to the universality of findings have been discussed earlier: similar national teacher-education programs, state teacher-certification requirements, textbooks, and age/grade achievement tests. One more factor comes into play. Many teachers formed their perceptions about Indians from the Westerns they saw as children. These links forge a universality connecting the Indian students of Madison to Indian students in the nation's public systems.

Throughout the nation, school districts are as ill-prepared to cope with the shifting sands of ethnic populations as was Madison.[1] Whether it is children of recent immigrants from Southeast Asia or Mexico affecting urban schools or the Indians in Madison, school districts are locked into outmoded teaching styles and curricula once thought appropriate for a homogenous student body. However, such teaching styles and curricula are not appropriate for heterogeneous and/or multiracial student populations.

The advantage of using Madison as a microcosm of national education is that both the school and the community were small enough to survey the school as a whole, a part of rather than apart from, a community. When community populations shift from homogenous to multiracial, and the power structure excludes rather than includes multiculturalism, schools resist change. School dis-

117

tricts are simply mirror images of communities. They use their energy and resources in ways that guarantee the quality of education will deteriorate for all students. In an increasingly multiracial society, excellence is inextricably woven into a multicultural educational tapestry. "At the level of the individual learner, [excellence] means performing on the boundary of individual ability. . . . In school and in the workplace, excellence characterizes a school or college that sets high expectations and goals for *all* learners, then tries in every way possible to help students reach that goal."[2]

That Madison had a problem became obvious after the classroom evaluations. The focus of the survey had more to do with attitudes than with education. The questions were designed to measure the perceptions of a need for change, resistance to change, and, concretely, whether the Madison school system was in concert or at odds with the Madison community. The survey questions were chosen organically from the initial interviews and classroom observations. In addition, some questions were included as a result of a literature search on multicultural education.

The following national educational studies were integrated into the Madison study to provide a balance between large and small educational systems:

A Nation at Risk, National Commission on Excellence, 1983
Action for Excellence, Task Force on Education for Economic Growth, 1985
Academic Preparation, The College Board, 1983
Making the Grade, Twentieth Century Fund, 1983.

All the teachers and both the principals took part in the survey. A yes/no scale in the teacher-principal survey was used to avoid a neutral response to some very sensitive questions.

The community survey was placed in each mailbox at the local post office where mail is delivered to Madison and reservation residents. Ninety Two responses came in, representing a 14 percent response rate. Of the ninety-two responses, 55.3 percent came from American Indians and 44.7 percent from non-Indians. This would seem an uneven distribution, except for the ratio of 70 percent Indian to 30 percent non-Indian students, meaning the non-Indian responses were disproportionate to the actual percentage of the non-Indian student body. Only those respondents who indicated that they had a child currently or recently attending the Madison schools were used in the survey.

The survey questions were formulated to clarify issues already identified through interviews and data. They were reduced to six areas of mutual concern.

1. The hiring policies and turnover rate both for teachers and for administrators.

2. Faculty sensitivity to Indian culture, concerns, and inclusion into the teaching staff.

3. Faculty teaching skills and the extent to which they recognized a need to upgrade skills and curriculum.

4. The extent to which faculty believed they had the materials and support necessary for excellent classroom teaching.

5. The discipline policy, and the use of corporal punishment.

6. Physical education in the school and extra-curricula sports activities after school.

While these were the dominant issues, the art program, the lack of a school nurse, the school library, and a number of other concerns surfaced during the on-site process. As a result, these issues were integrated into the survey questions.

The Hiring Policies and Turnover Rate Both for Teachers and for Administrators

At the time of this evaluation, the Madison School Board had been awarded approximately 1.2 million dollars from Impact Aid (874) funds for the construction of a new high school and basic operation. This is a great deal of money in a rural community where the allocation of contractors, the buying of building materials, and the hiring of workers over and above teachers, administrators, and supporting staff are based upon the school board's decision. The economic power school boards have over people's lives in a small community is awesome. They control the largest payroll and the most jobs and exercise more influence over community economics than even the local bank. Decisions they make are equally political and educational. The difficulty was separating out people's perceptions of whether the board decisions were primarily political or primarily educational.

The Madison board did not comfortably delegate authority, although the hiring of faculty was pro forma when the school superintendent made his recommendations. Board interest sharpened at one meeting when the employment of a bus driver and janitor was at stake. The school board members debated whether school policy should be to contract locally for building materials and contractors for the new high school. They questioned the superintendent intensely when he made his recommendations and displayed independence from their normal compliant routine. In all probability, they had personal knowledge of the applicants and a clearer understanding of the requirements for these jobs than for those of teachers.

The discussions showed sensitivity to the economic realities of the community. To give an example, the community survey participants reported an income range of zero to $40,000 with one quarter (25.4 percent) earning less than $5,000 annually and 5.6 percent earning $40,000 annually. Of the community survey pool (which excluded those connected with the school system), 30.6 percent indicated that they are professionals. At the same time, 67.1 percent were unemployed, meaning that for the vast majority any job would be a welcome respite from grinding poverty. Doling out even menial jobs, let alone the professional and contractual positions, placed a great deal of power in the hands of the board.

What were the perceptions of the faculty, principals, and community as to the wisdom of the school board decisions?

The school personnel are divided as to who should be hiring *all* school personnel (see figure 9.1). The board is elected by voters who believe they have common sense and a commitment to public education. Once seated, judgments are made equal to that of a CEO, without the prerequisite training. Were common sense and commitment sufficient in the eyes of the community at large to render wise decisions, or did the school board need training? The next question probes community perceptions of the administrative skills of the school board.

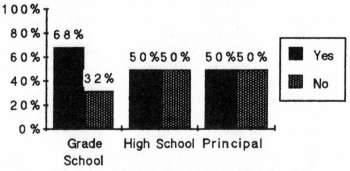

Figure 9.1 The School Board Should Hire All School Personnel

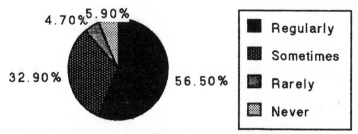

Figure 9.2 How Often Should the School Board Acquire Training to Improve Its Effectiveness?

More than half of the community at large indicated an uneasiness about the administrative experience of the school board. The overwhelming majority (90 percent) of the community survey respondents desired the school board members to enter into desired periodic or regular training to improve their effectiveness.

Seen as a whole, half of the school administrators, approximately two-thirds of the grade school faculty, half of the high school faculty, and more than half of the community at large agreed that the school board needed training to improve effectiveness. These assessments presuppose that people attend school board meetings. However, the survey found that almost two-thirds rarely, if ever, attend meetings. Evidently, the respondents either think all board members should receive training or they are getting negative information secondhand (see figure 9.2).

Board meetings are held at the Madison school. Would people be more actively involved if the meeting place alternated between the town and the reservation? The participants responded in about the same ratio as the racial makeup of the participants, that is, 55 percent Indian, 45 percent non-Indian.

Communication between the residents of the reservation and those of Madison has more to do with commerce than with camara-

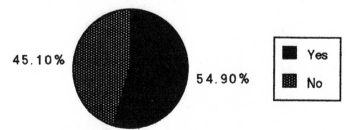

Figure 9.3 Should the School Board Rotate Monthly Meetings between the Reservation and Madison?

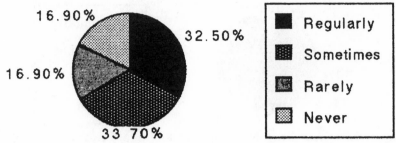

Figure 9.4 How Often Do You Attend a Social Activity on the Reservation?

derie. The reservation has cultural activities which two-thirds of the respondents report they have attended. The PTA meetings held in Madison are opportunities for parents from both communities to come together. Bearing in mind the ratio of 55/45 Indian to non-Indian, it seems that the majority of both communities, if given opportunities, would meet at least for social activities (see figures 9.3 to 9.6).

Indian participation is a requirement under the federal guidelines for receiving Impact Aid (874). The survey sought to assess community expectations of what "participation" consisted of Madison and the Indian communities were aware of the Department of Education's report. There was evidently heavy support to rectify the perfunctory role of the Indian Advisory Board to meet the standards set forth by federal regulations.

The communities overreacted to the criticism of the Department of Education because 67 percent wanted monthly meetings held with the 874 Indian Advisory Board. This is an unrealistic demand upon an unpaid five-member school board which also meets bimonthly with the school superintendent. The most efficient use of the school board time would be to delegate more authority to the superintendent. This is unlikely because of the high turnover

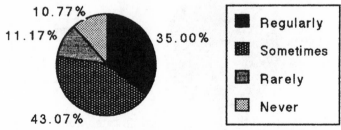

Figure 9.5 Would You Be Willing to Participate in the PTA?

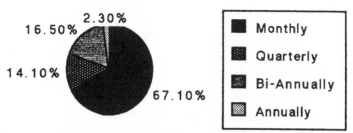

Figure 9.6 How Often Should the School Board, 874 Committee, and School Administrators Meet to Discuss School Business?

rate of this position. The distrust ripples down to the faculty and principals. While they are divided about whether the school board members, who are noneducators, should be hiring, they are equally divided about whether the superintendent or principals should have that authority. The survey also asked whether the faculty thought hiring school faculty ought to be left up to each school principal (see figures 9.7 and 9.8).

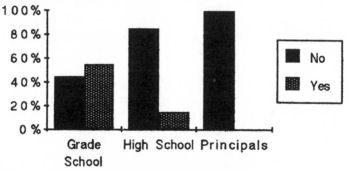

Figure 9.7 Should the Principal of Each School Hire All School Personnel within Each School?

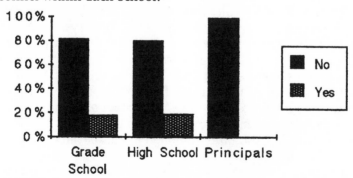

Figure 9.8 Should the School Superintendent Hire All School Personnel?

Notice the sharp division between the grammar-school faculty and the high-school faculty. Half of the senior faculty wanted all school personnel hired by the school board, but the grammar-school faculty placed greater trust in the professionalism of either the principal or the superintendent. Most of the newer faculty were employed in the grammar school. The responses of the two principals are confusing and are symptomatic of how they see their leadership role. Referring the first survey question, only one principal thought the school board should hire all school personnel, and yet both principals responded "no" to taking on that responsibility or allowing the superintendent to assume the responsibility. Ernest Boyer reported that this confusion existed nationally.[3] He proposed training and apprenticeship as a prerequisite for employment as a principal, but he said once hired they should

> have more control over their own budgets, operating within guidelines set by the District Officer. Further every principal should have a School improvement fund, discretionary money to provide time and materials for program development or for special seminars and staff retreats.

> Principals should also have more control over the selection and rewarding of teachers. Acting in consultation with their staffs, they should be given responsibility for the final choice of teachers for their schools.[4]

There is so much division between the school board, the faculty, the principals, and the superintendent as to who has or should have the authority to hire faculty that one can justifiably question how anyone gets hired or fired in the Madison school system. Actually, what happens is that whoever feels strongly about a prospective applicant usually carries the day with the school board, and since both principals have been reluctant to make their opinions known, the decision is ipso facto left to the superintendent to convince the school board. Once in a while, the school board overrides the superintendent, as was the case in the hiring of the high-school principal, with the result that although hired, she felt compelled to resign after only a year.

The next set of questions centered on the hiring practices in the Madison system and the extent to which there is a perception of racial bias in the hiring practices.

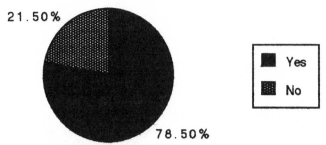

21.50%

78.50%

Figure 9.9 Does Racial Discrimination Occur in the Madison Schools?

Faculty Sensitivity to Indian Culture, Concerns, and Inclusion into the Teaching Staff

The most controversial aspect of this study was addressing the extent to which institutional racism exists, and if it does, the willingness of the Madison system to support remedies. Racism is unfashionable due to the civil rights movement, and yet it exists, transformed from the historical practice of individual racism to a collective form generally termed as "institutional racism." For the sake of clarity, and because there are so many definitions that people either reject or accept, for this book racism is defined as a dominant culture's withholding from a minority, power, prestige, and privilege.

To what extent were the allegations of racism made by the Indian community rooted in reality? The community survey asked whether racism was perceived in the Madison school system (see figure 9.9). Mindful of the ratio of approximately 55 percent Indian to 45 percent non-Indian, both races, or 78.5 percent, think that racism is evident in the school system.

A follow-up to that question concerns the frequency of the practice of racism (see figure 9.10).

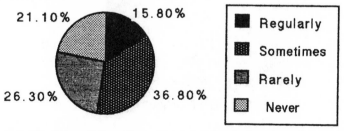

21.10%   15.80%

26.30%   36.80%

Figure 9.10 How Often Does Racial Discrimination Occur in the Clinton Schools?

Approximately the same percentage in the community survey felt that racism does not exist and responded "never," but of the 78.5 percent that felt racism does exist, nearly half felt it was evident most or some of the time. The next set of survey questions were to determine how much of the community perceptions are a mirror image of the Madison school system. The survey asked what is termed a "loaded question" because it opens the door to a critical appraisal of effective teaching. The previous chapters assessed academic standings of the school in relation to statewide achievement scores but left open the question of whether the existence of racism or a lack of knowledge about the multicultural student population contributed to the lackluster academic standings in the school system. The survey sought to assess the knowledge of or desire for understanding the Indian culture of most of the student body and the extent to which the entire school system was willing to adopt a multicultural faculty, curriculum, and knowledge about Indian culture (see figures 9.11 and 9.12).

Almost 90 percent of the faculty thought that learning about Indian culture was appropriate (see figure 9.13).

Three-quarters of the community study respondents felt that information about the reservation should be included during a three-day orientation session before the beginning of school in the fall.

Is a three-day orientation session sufficient to learn about Indian culture, or should Indian studies be included in the regular academic program?

About three-quarters of the community survey participants wanted Indian studies as a regular or sporadic academic discipline, evidence that non-Indians think their children should be exposed to knowledge about their Indian neighbors.

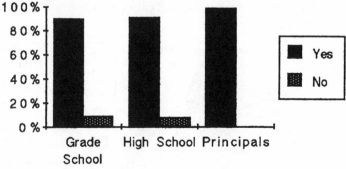

Figure 9.11 Should Faculty Be Knowledgeable about Indian Culture?

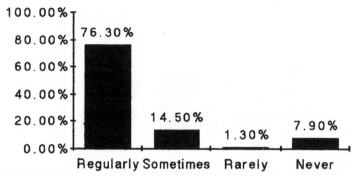

Figure 9.12 Should Orientation Include Information about the Indian Reservation?

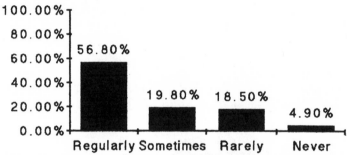

Figure 9.13 Should the Madison School District Offer Indian Studies and the History/Language of The Reservation?

The survey also tested out the extent to which the faculty and principals would support multicultural education with inclusion of Indian language in the academic program (see figure 9.14).

The identification of Indian language as a course presupposes the inclusion of Indian teachers, because teachers often suppose cultural courses can be taught by anyone, whereas language must be native taught. The most receptive to the inclusion of Indian language were the grammar-school teachers, with the high-school teachers and principals equally divided.

Studies conducted nationally support the inclusion of Indian language as part of a regular academic discipline: "This lack of respect, along with a disregard for students' languages and cultures in many schools enrolling Indian students both on and off reservations are contributing to the disappearance of tribal languages and identity. At the same time, they are having a devastating effect on school achievement and retention. To continue to ignore such issues is not acceptable."[5]

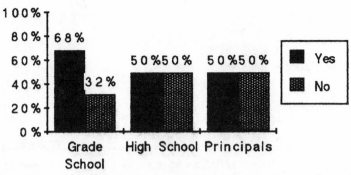

Figure 9.14 Should American Indian Language Be Taught in Clinton Schools?

Narrowing this further, do parents think children would learn an Indian language if it were offered?

Of the three-quarters who were receptive to the inclusion of studies/language/culture, 69 percent felt their children would participate (see figures 9.15 and 9.16).

Would these courses be attended sporadically or regularly as any other discipline, such as math or history?

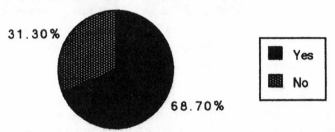

Figure 9.15 Would Your Child Participate in a Tribal Language/Culture Course If It Were Taught in School?

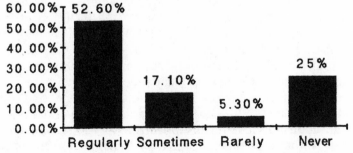

Figure 9.16 How Frequent Would Your Child Attend a Tribal Language/Culture Course If it Were Taught in the School?

More than half would attend Indian curricula on a regular basis, and another 17 percent would attend a class on a term-to-term basis. This is probably as good a reception one would expect for any nonrequired language course.

The survey questions relating to institutional racism drew the most controversy and contradiction. Reason dictates that the idea of replacing existing teachers in order to hire Indians is unpalatable. However, what would the response be to hiring Indian teachers when vacancies occur? This would not require firing of existing faculty, because in any given year, one-quarter, and in some years half, of the faculty are newcomers both to the school and to the field of teaching. In spite of that common knowledge, the survey sought to find out if the system saw the turnover rate as normal for a rural school.

Surprisingly, the same principals who stated in their interviews they needed to hire more Indian teachers and the teacher turnover rate was unusual even for a rural school responded negatively to the turnover survey question and positive to the hiring of Indian faculty.

Adding to the confusion of how the Madison system sees itself, the teachers see the turnover rate as high but do not think Indian teachers should replace existing vacancies, but the principals see the turnover rate as low and want to fill vacancies with Indian teachers (see figures 9.17 and 9.18). This is a small school where people know each other very well. Why the contradiction?

At first glance, the teachers and the administrators are at odds with each other. The teachers believe that Indian teachers will present a threat to their autonomy, both in the classroom and in the system. Five certified Indian teachers were employed in the tribal education department because they could not get a job working for the Madison system. In addition, the community survey found that

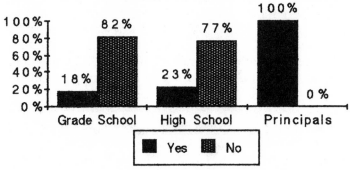

Figure 9.17 Is the Teacher Turnover Rate Normal When Compared to That in Other Rural Schools in the State?

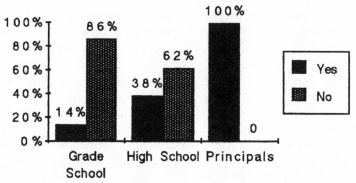

Figure 9.18 As Faculty Leave, Should They Be Replaced by Certified American Indian Teachers?

34 percent of the respondents had completed college, and 13 percent held a master's degree. The principals in this system were not delegated to hire teachers. The school board, upon recommendation from the superintendent, hired teaching personnel.

Preserving institutional racism—withholding power, prestige, and privilege from the Indians—has been costly to the Madison system. It has deprived the school of a stable faculty and a cultural bridge between two races. The deterioration of the quality of education is directly attributable to these two factors.

Comparison of Madison schools to others in the nation leads to the conclusion that institutional racism exists in many school systems. The National Coalition of Advocates for Students found that many schools were

> unwilling to implement affirmative action policies that would diversify the teaching and administrative staff, including persons more representative of the racial and cultural minorities served by the schools. As a school desegregation officer said in Boston "We must have multicultural models in the schools if we are to shatter the myth of minority inferiority and white superiority. . . . Children have to function in a multi-cultural world."[6]

There is an unspoken premise that Indians, even those certified, are somehow less prepared academically because of university affirmative action. This is generally couched in terms of "lowering the standards." The reality is that diversity improves equity and excellence. *A Nation at Risk* asserted:

We do not believe that a public commitment to excellence and educational reform must be made at the expense of a strong public commitment to the equitable treatment of our diverse population. The twin goals of equity and high quality schooling have profound and practical meaning for our economy and society, and we cannot permit one to yield to the other in principle or in practice. To do so would deny young people their chance to learn and live according to their aspirations and abilities. It would also lead to a generalized accommodation to mediocrity in our society on the one hand or the creation of an undemocratic elitism on the other.[7]

Faculty Teaching Skills and the Extent to Which They Recognized a Need to Upgrade Skills and Curricula

Good teachers are lifelong learners. For them, teaching is a profession, and like any profession, it demands continual training to keep up with the field. Educational systems generally provide in-service training to keep teachers current in their discipline.

During the interview stage it was evident that some teachers felt frustrated with their current level of skill, so the survey sought to find out the extent to which in-service training was desired (see figure 9.20).

The principals saw the need to bring in-service training, but one-third of the grade-school and almost one half of the high-

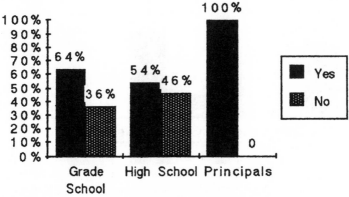

Figure 9.20 Is More In-service Training Needed?

school teachers did not feel the necessity for in-service training. An indication of how far afield the faculty are comes from a study conducted nationally.

> We cannot expect a teacher trained twenty years ago to prepare students to live forty years into the future with no policy of systematic continued education for the teacher. Even the most dedicated teacher will fall behind, and the students will learn how to live, not in the future, but in the past. School boards must accept lifelong learning as an essential condition for every teacher.
>
> A Two Week Teacher Professional Development Term should be added to the school year, with appropriate compensation. This term for teachers would be a time for study, a period to improve instruction and to expand knowledge. The planning of such a term should be largely controlled by teachers at the school or district level.[8]

Many states require postcertification courses either for license renewal or in some systems for salary step increases. The vast majority favored taking a course every five years in their field (see figure 9.21). The fact that the faculty opposed in-service training but supported university course work may be because the in-service training provided previously was inadequate or because they were given no choice as to the subject or the instructor.

The Madison participants are in agreement with the national studies to improve educational quality: "Every five years, teachers should be eligible to receive a special contract—with extra pay to match—to support a Summer Study Term. To qualify and compete

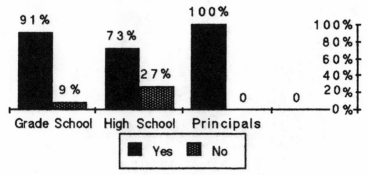

Figure 9.21 Should Faculty Take at Least Three Units of Credit Every Five Years to Keep Current in Their Field?

for this extended contract, each teacher would prepare a study plan. Such a plan would be subject to review and approval both by peers and by the school and district administrations."[9]

The institution of education is in a dynamic continuum, each decade finding fault with the one preceding it. It has not yet been resolved whether systems and/or teachers should be held responsible for student achievement. It may be impossible to resolve this issue until such time as the nation as a whole makes education a priority and supplies potential teachers with excellent training and supports them with excellent texts and teaching materials, including computers, satellite systems in the classroom, and lifelong education through in-service training and educational sabbaticals.

Nonetheless, many argue that the teaching profession is the only one not held accountable for its product. If lawyers lost as many cases as teachers lose students, or doctors lost as many patients on the operating table, some credentialing agency somewhere would sit up and take notice. Do Madison teachers see themselves accountable for their students' achievement? (See figure 9.22.)

There seemed to be virtually universal agreement that teachers should not be accountable for student achievement. In truth, almost every study on education agrees with this point of view, although private schools would totally disagree. Private schools expect their students to achieve excellence, because there is money on the line. This Pygmalion effect transfers from administrators to teachers and from teachers to students. Public education argues that the funding for excellence available in private institutions is not available to them, and consequently they are working at a considerable disadvantage.

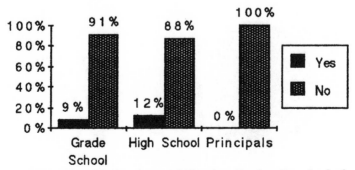

Figure 9.22 Should the Annual Teacher Evaluation Include the Student SRA Scores as One Measure of Effectiveness?

Language Requirements

The world is in rapid change, and *global village* is more than just a term coined by Buckminster Fuller. The acquisition of language skills is increasingly important and takes on new importance for the next generation. Many colleges anticipate the need for language acquisition and require prior high-school language courses to qualify for admission. The Madison system did not have language courses, but the community was aware of the impending modifications of the language requirement for college entry. The community survey overwhelmingly supported the inclusion of a foreign language into the curriculum (see figure 9.23).

It is understandable that Madison could not afford to offer a range of language classes. This state borders on Canada, where French is spoken. Spanish has risen in importance nationally in terms of commerce and communication. The Madison community and school were asked to make some choices.

About two-thirds of the community felt French should be taught. In Madison, the high-school faculty and principal but not the grammar-school faculty, supported the inclusion of French into the curriculum.

There was even greater community support for the inclusion of Spanish into the Madison curriculum (see figures 9.24 to 9.27).

The grade-school faculty and principal did not support language as an academic study before high school. In reality, the most opportune time to introduce a second language is in grammar school. At that age children learn quicker and retain more because they enjoy learning a second language: "Every public school student should start the study of a foreign language in elementary school which is standard educational practice in the developed countries

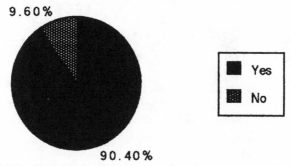

Figure 9.23   Should the Madison School System Teach a Foreign Language?

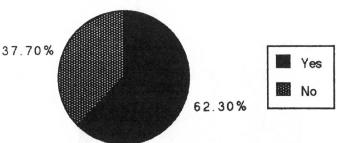

Figure 9.24 Should the Madison School Offer French?

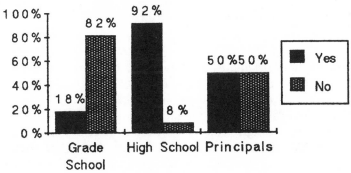

Figure 9.25 Should French Be Taught in the Madison School System?

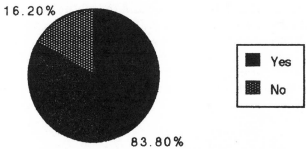

Figure 9.26 Should the Madison School Offer Spanish?

of the world. A knowledge of a second language at an early age will stimulate a better appreciation of our country's cultural pluralism. The achievement of proficiency in a second language must be a project for this decade, not for future generations."[11]

The acquisition of a foreign (or, in this case, domestic) language is a foothold into multiculturalism as well as essential for navigation into a global world. It was impressive how much consen-

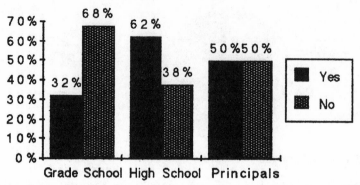

Figure 9.27 Should Spanish Be Taught in the Madison School System?

sus about language inclusion came from the Madison faculty as well as the community at large. There was only a difference of opinion as to whether language should be acquired in grammar school or in high school. In the community survey, 90 percent of the community thought that a foreign language should be taught. More than 60 percent thought the foreign language should be French, while more than 80 percent thought Spanish ought to be taught. There was substantial support for the inclusion of Indian language by more than half of the grammar and high school faculty and the community. The Indian students are multicultural. They speak English, and if they are not fluent in Indian, they understand it, because the elders in their family speak Indian daily. The non-Indian students are educationally deprived because they will be entering to world equipped with a myopic understanding of that world. The overwhelming response to the inclusion of language into the curriculum appears to have fallen on deaf ears, because there was no indication of hiring faculty with this expertise.

The Extent to Which Faculty Believed They Had the Materials and Support Necessary for Excellent Classroom Teaching

Budget crunches notwithstanding, there is a bottom line to support teaching excellence. Textbooks and library resources must be current, and simple things such as copy machines and ditto paper have to be available. Madison did not have a single computer in the classroom, nor did anyone consider purchasing a satellite system or any other technological advances that support teaching excellence.

Rural teachers do not live in a vacuum. They are aware of better, more advanced texts in their subject. Madison teachers were asked whether the texts they were using were the best available in their subject (see figure 9.28).

Slightly more than half responded, saying "yes." However, this is at variance with an analysis of textbooks conducted by the National Coalition of Advocates for Students who argued that textbooks needed considerable overhauling:

> Surprisingly, few school systems have made investments in revising curriculum to reflect the variety of cultures in the nation and in the world. Witnesses told us of Native American children sitting through lessons about "taming the frontier" and of Columbus "discovering America," of world history texts which devote no more than a few paragraphs to Africa; of Asian history courses that all Japanese, Chinese, and Filipino people, whose histories are all different and all need to be told; of schools in the Southwest which teach the history of their region with little more than a cursory look at its rich pre-Anglo culture. Such accounts reminded us again and again of how devastating it can be for students to attend schools which "disconfirm rather than confirm their histories, experiences and dreams."[10]

I have been on a textbook panel for the State of California which was empowered to read, accept, or reject textbooks for use in

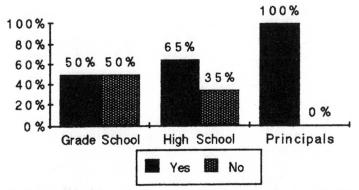

Figure 9.28 Would You Change Some Textbooks in My Subject Area If You Could?

the public school systems within the state. The most widely accepted publishers woefully neglect the inclusion of racial and ethnic minorities in the texts, even now with perfunctory paragraphs or even some chapters that do not reveal the whole truth about the racial history of the United States. For instance, the widely used textbooks about California's history ignore the fact that 90 percent of the Californian Indians were killed in northern California during the gold rush, Indian slavery was state sanctioned by the California legislation, and Junipero Sera enslaved Indians to build his missions and consequently thousands of Indians were mutilated after running away and being caught or died because of the conditions during the mission period.

As a professor of American Indian studies I have taught students about federal-Indian relations that should be basic knowledge acquired in grammar school. I have taught ethnic studies and find that college students even today are incredulous to find out about the Japanese internment camps, Jim Crow laws in the South, and even the civil rights movement. Anyone who has taught college-level ethnic studies knows students come to class with very little knowledge of multicultural history. Worse yet, racial and linguistic minorities go through twelve years of schooling without any understanding of how much their culture has contributed toward the development of the richness of this country. Textbooks should be completely rewritten to include the art, science, literature, and history of minorities in this country.

Physical Education in the Madison School, and Extra Curricular Sports Activities

Textbooks are very important, but art and physical education programs channel creativity and energy and significantly support educational excellence. These two subjects are highly valued in the Indian community. Even Indians who live on or below the poverty line proudly display original Indian art on their walls, and families sacrifice a great deal to provide children with art materials. Athletics is, for many Indians, the chief means of support in college and status on the reservation. As mentioned earlier, these two fields were dropped from Madison's grade-school budget.

At Madison, art and physical education classes started at the junior-high level. The grade-school principal commented that P.E. in the grade school was unnecessary and that teachers who took their students out to the yard were sloughing off their academic assignments. Grade-school teachers felt that it was important to give students time away from their desks precisely because of their youth and energy. While the wisdom of excluding physical education in the primary level is disputed, there is strong faculty support for an art program (see figure 9.29).

Discipline

Aside from academics, student discipline is a highly controversial issue in any school system. In the Madison system, teachers complained that fighting, rowdiness, drugs, and alcohol have contributed significantly to the deterioration of education. There seems to be a national consensus that these problems exist, but the remedies run the gamut ranging from dismissal to aggressive parent-teacher-student counseling. One study reported:

> It became clear to us in our inquiry that suspensions are used more extensively in some schools with little evidence that this is an effective technique for encouraging good discipline. This practice also raises questions about how seriously schools value academic instruction. Students who are not in class can hardly keep up with an academic program. The detrimental effect on the education of a student who is suspended is obvious.

> Suspension means kids are outside on the street, ready to fight. It makes no sense, for example, to suspend a kid for alcohol or drugs and then offer no drug program in the school.

The use of suspension in public schools is frequent, but few

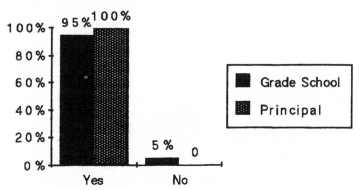

Figure 9.29 Would an Art Program Improve Education at the Madison Grade School?

suspensions are for dangerous behavior. From our witnesses we learned of school districts in which out-of-school suspensions are frequently used for class cutting, tardiness, and truancy, despite the fact that this punishment does little, if anything, to deal with those symptoms of limited motivation. A witness who works with truants in New York City stated the suspension issue quite simply . . . "The more days of school one misses, the further behind one gets, and the harder it is to go back and keep going back." Suspension is not an appropriate or effective tool for breaking this cycle.[12]

The faculty perception of the Indian students was that they engaged in disruptive classroom behavior brought about through the use and abuse of alcohol. Young Indians often do have firsthand experience of alcoholism in their immediate or extended family. However, because tribes have aggressive alcoholic prevention programs, this generation of Indians has fewer numbers engaging in excessive drinking or drugs. The Indian community alleged that their youth were victims of stereotyping by the Madison school system. They were especially alarmed when the high-school faculty pushed a system-wide discipline policy through the school board which placed heavy reliance upon suspension.

Community members, particularly Indians, complained that discipline was not meted out in an even-handed manner. They alleged that Indian children, often taller and heavier than white children of the same age came under harsher discipline than non-Indians of the same age. Others felt that rowdiness in the school yard was handled differently if it involved Indian children with Indian children, or Indian children with non-Indians (see figures 9.30 to 9.35).

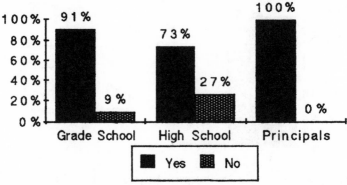

Figure 9.30 Is the School Discipline Policy Fair and Workable?

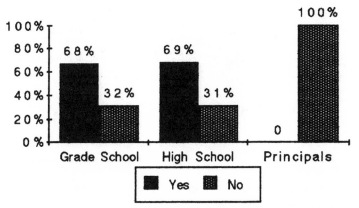

Figure 9.31 Do the Faculty Know Most of the Students' Parents?

The general agreement throughout the school system was that the policy was fair and workable. This was at odds with the feelings of community members who complained that the policy was not fair and punishment was meted out unevenly to the Indian students. I observed during one confrontation in the school yard between an Indian student and a white student that the Indian student was put on suspension, while the non-Indian student was lectured by the school principal. The reason given was that the argument was started by the Indian student. However, both students were fighting in the school yard.

Fairness is difficult to achieve unless schools know both the child and the parents. How much communication was there from classroom to home? The teachers/principals were asked whether they knew most of the parents of their students.

If a child was in trouble, what steps were taken to engage parental support in seeking solutions? Were parents notified of any disciplinary action taken?

Almost half of the parents were not notified by teachers or

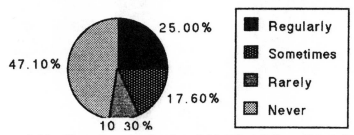

Figure 9.32 How Frequently Am I Notified When Disciplinary Action Is Taken against My Child in the Madison Schools?

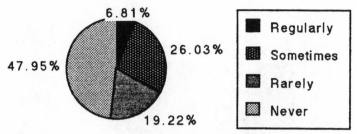

Figure 9.33 How Frequently Do I Meet With the School Guidance Counselors?

principals when disciplinary action was taken. Were they notified by the guidance counselors?

How serious was the discipline problem? What are the perceptions of drug and alcohol as behavioral contributing factors?

It is surprising to find that teachers perceive drugs and alcohol as a major problem in the grammar school and a minor one in the high school, especially since the Discipline Policy gained its momentum from the senior high school faculty. Are drugs and alcohol creating a discipline problem in the classroom? (See figures 9.34 to 9.36.)

The survey response is paradoxical, since student alcohol usage normally coincides with behavioral problems. If these problems exist, would parents support an alcohol or drug prevention program in the school?

The community apparently felt a need for a drug or alcohol prevention program in the school. Although 65 percent felt the students would attend a prevention program regularly, the vast majority, more than 90 percent felt that students would attend a

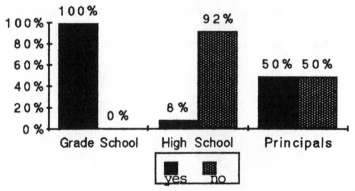

Figure 9.34 Are Drugs and Alcohol a Serious Problem in the Madison School?

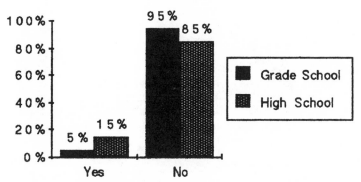

Figure 9.35 Do Teachers Have a Hard Time Handling Discipline in Class?

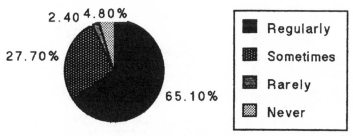

Figure 9.36 If the School Had a Drug and Alcohol Abuse Prevention Program, How Often Would Your Child Attend?

prevention program at some time. Indian and non-Indian alike perceived alcohol in particular and drugs secondarily as a potential problem for all students.

There was some discussion about corporal punishment in the school. This is surprising, since teachers felt that discipline was not a problem in their classroom. It is against state law to exercise corporal punishment. Nonetheless, the questions were asked to see how strongly faculty felt about the issue (see figures 9.37 and 9.38).

Almost two-thirds of the teaching faculty thought corporal punishment should be allowed. This attitude would lead to extreme volatile reaction from the community, especially the Indian community. Should corporal punishment be strictly the principal's domain?

Here we have an explosive combination. Principals do not know the parents of the students. Parents are not notified when disciplinary action is taken against their children. Guidance counselors do not reach out to parents. And the Madison faculty/administrators feel that principals should be able to exercise corporal punishment.

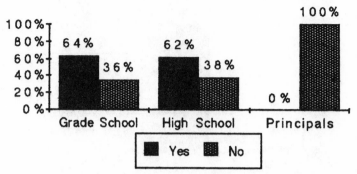

Figure 9.37   Should Teachers Have the Right to Exercise Corporal Punishment in Extreme Cases of Student Misbehavior?

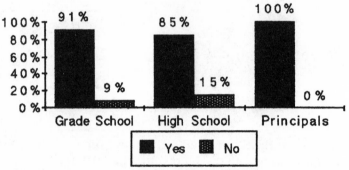

Figure 9.38   Should the Principal Have the Right to Exercise Corporal Punishment in Extreme Cases of Misbehavior?

Madison offers few if any forums for social or athletic activities. Young people "hang out" with little to do after school, providing fertile opportunity for trouble. One of the criticisms hurled at the Madison system was the absence of extracurricular activities. Parents commented that sheer isolation from intellectual or physical facilities almost certainly played a large role in behavioral problems. The reservation was equally remiss in providing recreational after-school activities because it had a large indoor heated swimming pool (sometimes closed because of budgetary constraints) and teen center.

Extracurricular Activities

The principals were unanimous in feeling that Madison needed a supervised after-school program for *most* of the students. Cur-

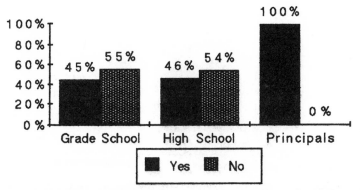

Figure 9.39 Should There Be a Supervised After-School Program for Most of the Students?

rently, male, athletically gifted students are on school athletic teams, but many students were left out of activities. Half of the faculty did not agree that there should be an after school program. They may have been concerned about *who* would have the responsibility or whether these activities would be at the expense of classroom materials.

The community survey indicates that there is some correlation between their concerns and those of the faculty.

The next community survey indicates that there is division about after-school activities as well (see figures 9.39 to 9.44).

There were two outlets for students in the community. One was the school gym, the other the reservation swimming pool. The survey sought to find out how accessible or desirable these resources were for the students.

Over one-half of the community and school faculty agree that there should be after-school activities. The reservation swimming pool offers the best opportunity for a cross-section of ages and popu-

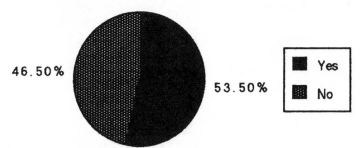

Figure 9.40 Are You Satisfied with the Madison School District Extra Curricular Activities?

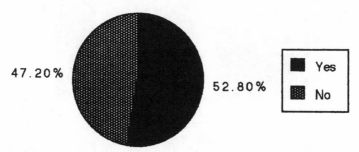

Figure 9.41 Would You Like to Have More After-School Activities for Your Children?

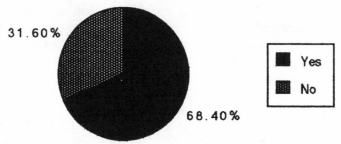

Figure 9.42 Is the Madison Gym Available to Students After School?

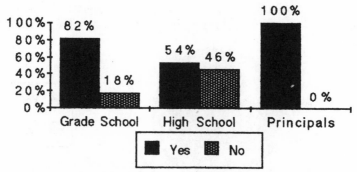

Figure 9.43 Should Madison Schools Contract with the Reservation for the Use of the Swimming Pool to Augment the Physical Education Program?

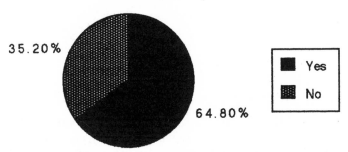

35.20%

Yes
No

64.80%

Figure 9.44 Should the Reservation Have Its Own Swim Team?

lations to markedly reduce the racial isolation in this area. Both races encounter each other in the school and do business in the town, but these are essentially mandatory encounters. The swimming pool on the reservation represents a voluntary encounter where students and parents alike have a meeting ground. Consider the ratio of fifty-five to forty-five Indian/non-Indian and it appears that about 10 percent of non-Indians felt that a swim team would be beneficial for young people.

Extra-curricular activities allow each population to compete and cooperate, and in this system appeared to be at a minimum. Schools have a choice. They can be a community resource for recreational as well as social, business, and economic meeting grounds, or they can close their doors after three o'clock and separate from the community. The best chance both town, school, and reservation have to reduce or obliterate racial isolation is using the meager recreational resources to bring people together.

Alumni Survey

In the end, the graduates must take what they received from school and forge ahead. Eighteen graduates were interviewed, and these are their unedited responses. They were asked opened-ended questions. Some choose not to answer every question, and others gave several responses to the same question. They represent eloquent testimony to the desire of Madison students to receive quality and equitable education.

What areas do you think need to be improved at the high school? Examples: sports related, academic, administration related, food related, bussing, library , etc.

Responses:

1. All.

2. Math.

3. Administration.

4. More emphasis on academic and vocational education.

5. I think the food program should become better, the menus should be changed every week—the cooks should cook better—more language courses also make the school more academically oriented rather than the sports oriented.

6. A stronger firmer administration would help in dealing with discipline problems.

7. It is about time that the reservation be given a fair representation of seats on the school board, the numbers say we should have three.

8. Attitude-enthusiasm, caring, sharing.

9. Teachers need to take more of a concern for the students especially the Indian student. Teachers should make the Indian students feel wanted and confident like they belong.

10. Most positive image problems for our students is leadership, self-awareness.

11. Administration, I personally feel the Indian students are treated differently from that of the non-Indian students.

12. Sports should be pushed a little harder with grades. Council could be better in their decisions and let the students in on the answers.

13. Administration, that are not consistent. The emphasis must be placed on education.

Other comments or suggestions that you think will help us to improve the quality of education in Madison schools.

1. There is a need for Native American Input (school board).

2. More Indians on the School Board.

3. Classes on Drugs and Alcohol.

4. Let new teachers form their own opinion of Native Americans—good or bad.

5. Firm action in handling their discipline problems will result in firmer control of the students in the classroom which will result in a more controlled academic setting.

6. Obstacles will always exist as long as Madison and the reservation refuse to accept each other as people. Madison has to accept us as equals and the reservation has to quit taking so much for granted.

7. Total administration change to include all personnel, staff, teachers, janitors, etc.

8. I think the new school in Madison would definitely improve the education for the younger people to reach high school.

9. Get quality teachers and quality administrators. Implement some modern methods of education.

10. Show the Indian students that they have the abilities to become successful and educated.

11. More Native American teachers who identify with problems of Indian children.

12. More cultural awareness of classes for non-Indians, teachers.

13. More discipline.

14. I would like to see classes offered as an elective to help the younger children in areas such as common courtesy, social graces, grooming.

15. Some more courses offered would be nice.

16. If the administration could get along with the teachers.

17. There should be more support for the Indian Club there and more people should join it in order to have a successful pow wow.

18. Try to get more tutoring to the students who need it most.

19. Good teachers are needed who will challenge their students. Emphasis must be placed on quality education. I got to college and was not prepared in the specific area of foreign language, math and science.

20. More classes need to be offered in foreign language, economics, history, geography, computer science, and science.

In the previous chapters, the study showed that small class size notwithstanding, students in the Madison system were not measuring up to the state average. ABT and other studies would have stopped there, but we hypothesized that the outcomes of education are directly related to the institutional racism within the school and community. The survey in this chapter sought to expose the extent to which institutional racism played a part in the disintegration of education in the Madison school system by examining hiring policy and turnover rate, faculty sensitivity to Indian culture or multiculturalism, faculty skills and curriculum used, appropriate classroom materials from the perspective of the teachers, and the discipline policy. Rather than rely solely upon statistical data as did the ABT study, the Madison survey incorporated the communities both of reservation and of the town of Madison with the faculty and administrative surveys.

What the survey showed is a strong resistance to acknowledging the unique culture of Indian students in the hiring practices even though the turnover rate was appreciably higher than that of most systems. The ambiguous leadership role of the superintendent, principals, and school board allows each party to obscure responsibility for inclusion of multiculturalism in the faculty or curriculum. Moreover, the chasm between the school, the town, and the reservation even in the inclusion of language (Indian or foreign), utilizing the school and reservation recreational facilities with an after-school program, eliminating art, and the discipline policy contributes significantly to the conflict between the two races.

There is substantial dissatisfaction with the Madison school system, but the school alone is not to blame. The institutional racism in the Madison community is reflected in the Madison school system. The often frustrating on-site observances of Madison's classrooms coupled with community surveys illuminates, with frightening clarity, the incontrovertible impact of institutional racism as the predominant cause of the deterioration of education in this country. If the predominantly white communities in this nation want better education for their children, they will have to change. Without strong visionary leadership from the government, the community power elite, school administrators and school boards, the outcome is not promising.

10

The Legacy of Institutional Racism

My grandfather, a tall, wily old Indian whose weathered face was like a map of Indian Country, loved to gamble. Win or lose, he used to say "Timing is everything." As I am writing this final revision, Herrnstein and Murray have come up with another attack on the intelligence of African Americans.[1] Newt Gingrich and others suggest the key to reversing current trends in teenage and/or unmarried pregnancies is to put the offspring in orphanages, and California's Proposition 187 was passed denying education and health care to illegal aliens. Hooray for timing! The events may sadden, unfuriate, or gladden the reader, but they are also grist for the mill for the main idea of this book.

The focus of this study is to illustrate the ways that institutional racism in our communities negatively constrains educational excellence in our schools. All of the above (Hernstein and Murray, Newt Gingrich and others, and Proposition 187) signal changes in American social policy divorced from the institutional racism that caused the problems to begin with. Generated by statistical evidence, detached from everyday life of the underclass in our communities, they seek to eliminate the symptoms, not the disease.

There are many eminent social scientists expert in conducting studies that illuminate social problems. Some of them have even found their way into the national spotlight. But these studies rarely are translated into national social policy because most of them offer solutions that inevitably lead to resolving and reversing centuries of entrenched institutional racism in American communities. The nation would benefit if the underclass received the education and

151

resources to lead productive lives, but corporate and political power would stand to lose as their hold on the economy eroded. Institutional racism did not begin in this century or the last, but from the very beginning of U.S. history, as African Americans were defined as three-fifths human.

In 1790 the federal government passed the Naturalization Act, limiting citizenship to whites only. Clearly, this was a signal to people of color they were unwelcome, or at least to be kept away from power, prestige, and privlege. As the poor overwhelmed our cities, Congress and state legislators responded by building bigger orphanages, which even Theordore Roosevelt found a grievous response to addressing the needs of the poor when he sought to close down these institutions. To address cultural differences of Indian people we had off-reservation boarding schools and the Dawes Allotment Act. The slavery policy, the Dred Scot decision, the Chinese Exclusion Act of 1882, and the Japanese Internment Act all addressed a national racial social policy, much the same as Proposition 187. Many of these policies were generated by statistics, compiled by those in power to remain in power.

Today we are still using statistical measurements to validate the claim that black intelligence or Indian culture are to blame for poverty and illiteracy rather than compelling the nation's Amer-Euro ethnocentrics to examine and remedy the role they play in contributing to these social problems.[2] It is agreed that we need to accept far more personal responsibility for our lives. Inescapable as well is the fact that in any given week newspaper headlines report drug wars and drive-by shootings alongside the irresponsible (and oftimes criminal) behavior of major corporations such as General Motors, Kerr McGee, Exxon, General Electric, S and Ls, not to mention the Canadian corporation that paid the U.S. treasury $20,000 for the right to mine $5 billion worth of gold in Nevada. As a nation, if we exact personal responsibility for the most vulnerable, surely we should exhort the same standards for the elite.

And why are all these forces coming together now as opposed to five or ten years ago? Because the power elite, the dominant white society, feels its grasp on social instutitions eroding or at least being seriously undermined by cultural pluralism. In his introduction to his book *From Distance Shores*, Ronald Takaki reports that even *Time Magazine* in a 1990 cover story reported that white Americans will be a minority group by the year 2056 and that California today leads the way with whites being 58 percent of the population. In a perverse way, the events mentioned signal the growing influence of cultural pluralism because power never reacts with such visible force unless it is threatened. Only a fool uses a cannon to anihilate a mosquito.

Hernstein and Murray, like ABT, relied solely on statistics to make their case that African Americans do not follow the normal bell curve, but rather the curve is skewed for lower intelligence than the average found in white dominant society. This study is dangerous not so much for what it says but because it offers American society comfort in blaming the cause of the decline of the American social fabric on minorities. The ABT study did the same thing with American Indian students, divorcing itself from the everyday life of Indian children as they cope with institutional racism inherent in American society. Does anyone seriously think that American Indian, African American, or Chicano children typically receive the same kind of education as their white counterparts in the same school by the same teachers? If so, they have never sat in a classroom and watched the signals teachers give to students based upon their assumption (albeit subconscious or stereotypic) of innate ability. What contributions did racism make toward designing the tests used, writing and publishing the curriculum in the nation's schools, training the teachers. Hernstein and Murray would have us believe that their study is uncontaminated by social factors.

Newt Gingrich and others have argued publically on talk shows that the statistics show that the disintegration of family values can best be remedied by placing children in orphanages or at least forcing welfare mothers to accept any job within two years of being on welfare. There is something diabolically contradictory about espousing family values and eschewing abortion and at the same time suggesting the placement of children in orphanages.[3] Again, statistics are used to validate their claim that this nation is brim full of parasites that need to learn the work ethic, ignoring their own federal studies conducted by the Health and Human Services Department as well as the National Child Welfare League in Washington, D.C., that 70 percent of welfare mothers go off of welfare under their own volition within two years of their first welfare check. They return to the welfare system because they cannot afford child care and health care with minimum wage salaries, often the only work for which they are qualified. Again, statistics are not very illuminating because they do not examine the role institutional racism has played in the lives of minorities, from renting a place to live, to finding a job, to receiving the training they need, or for that matter, for the state's lackluster role in forcing fathers to support their children. I was one of these unfortunate thousands of woman, but the difference was that I was lucky enough to come under

Johnson's War on Poverty. One of the programs paid my way through college, and from there I was supported through graduate school by the Bureau of Indian Affairs and the Office of Indian Education. What these mothers need is a chance and choice, but for that one has to examine the social fiber of a society that has denied them both.

Proposition 187 is a look at statistics without the concomitant examination of social institutions that have served to pull illegal aliens into their web while at the same time exploit cheap labor. These poor unfortunate people are attracted by the magnet of work U.S. citizens would not take at often less than minimum wage, sweat shops in our garment industry that produce clothes of our most prestigious designers, and corporate farms who need the stoop labor and are unwilling to pay living wages. By this piece of legislation, we are denying children basic health care and education.

The bedrock of cultural pluralism began with the American Indian tribes' initial encounters with white settlers. While tribes were open to cultural enchange, the settlers were myopic to the values intrinsic in tribal societies. They instead focused on the confiscation of native land and the piracy of native crops, which they converted into capitalism.[4] As early as the 1800s property and wealth secured the exclusive right of whites to become citizens, vote, receive an education, own a business and property, and become the foundation of institutional racism.[5] The foundation of institutional racism was the development of political, social, and economic institutions to deny the humanity and equality of the Indian tribes initially and all races later.[6] Rather than challenge the role these insitutions have played in our current social disfunction, these same institutions promote, provide for, and sanction statistical studies to validate their assertion that the victims of poverty and illiteracy are to blame for their own poverty and illiteracy.

So far, no one has produced a study denegrating the intelligence of the American Indian (although Terman did think the best that Indians could achieve was to be trained to be "efficient workers," but social scientists have not supported his view). What they have come up with, as discussed in chapter 1, are studies that lay the blame for Indian student underachievement on tribal culture, a culture they assert thwarts achieving academic excellence Terman states: "The whole question of racial differences in mental traits will have to be taken up anew . . . there will be discovered enormously significant racial differences . . . which cannot be wiped out of any schemes of mental culture. Children of this group should be segregated in special classes . . . they cannot master abstractions, but they can often be made efficient workers."[7]

The substance of this study is to illustrate the legacy institutional racism bequeaths to education. Described as a "sleepy little town," Madison is a socio-educational window into the dynamics of institutional racism. In this study, Madison defined community control as the exclusion of Indian representation in school governance because the town of Madison was predominantly white. When the entire community was examined it became clear that the school anthem of community control was a mirror image of the institutional racism within Madison. The ABT study contrasts sharply with the Madison study because ABT studied Indian education as if it were divorced from the ethos of the communities. This is the model most people use and accept, but it does not get at the problem or offer us any solution. Madison is a microcosim of the nation. The businesses may have been modest when viewed in terms of General Electric or Citibank Corp., but they acted in much the same way corporate interests behave throughout the nation. In Madison, they excluded the Indians from power, prestige, or privlege, while in New York or Los Angeles, other minorities are excluded or, at best, sparsely represented in the city power structure or school systems. Madison of course welcomed the buying power of tribal paychecks or Indian welfare checks. In cities throughout the nation, small and large businesses, apartment rentals, and medical professionals all exploit the buying power of minorities. The political power in the hands of the Madison City Council, the mayor, and school board resisted any inclusion of Indian representation which affected the educational level of all students, their own sons and daughters, as well as the Indian students. The same can be said for any city in the country with a sizeable minority population. The educational system reflected the interests and ethos of the exclusionary policies of the body politic and business. Inclusion of Indian representation through the election process was only possible because of the implicit threat of losing money, yet unless or until the community changes its institutional racism ethos, it is unlikely any real systemic change will take place in the school. With all the new social policies being bandied about by Gingrich, Murray, Hernstein, and Wilson as remedies of our national malaise, it should be blatently obvious that we cannot build enough prisons or orphanages to change the growing rage and social disfunction unless and until institutional racism is seen as being as unhealthy for society as smoking. Without that change, the nation's schools and our "sleepy little town of Madison," will deteriorate.

You can measure student achievement in a school, but that does not shed light on the realities of why schools fail children. For instance, it does not show that our schools, even in remote rural Madison, are changing from racially and culturally homogeneous to heterogeneous. The fact is that this phenomenon is measurably accelerating as new waves of migrants enter the nation's schools and traditional minorities, the African Americans and American Indians, attend public schools heretofore attended exclusively by white students. Studies that look at the framework and not the center (the classroom, faculty, school board, and community) cannot identify or offer solutions to the social cancer confronting the nation's schools. Madison is not an aberration of an American town confronting racial pluralism. The once stable homogeneous community is a creature of the past, and one could substitute Madison with thousands of small and large cities and find the same pattern. American urban and rural schools are the battleground where resistance to integrating multiculturalism in the community is played out in the governance and/or faculty of local schools.

The Madison study offers substantial evidence that institutional racism negatively affected the quality of education in Madison. Tracking the GPA of eleventh graders over a three-year period, showed that the average Madison student had a 2.47, meaning that even the 30 percent white student population did not achieve at a level commensurate with the state norms.

Madison employed one Indian teacher out of a faculty/staff of sixty and a student population of 70 percent Indian. The Indian presence within the system is overwhelmingly seen as janitors, bus drivers, aides, and kitchen staff, imprinting on the minds of young children that Indians are not destined to become professionals. Curricula that excluded knowledge about American Indians was detrimental to the quality of education for all students, because children need to learn more about cultural diversity if they are to navigate in a global world.

Madison's power elite, the decision-makers—the school board, mayor, and owners of businesses and the town bank—effectively locked out minority representation in the power structure. The institutional racism (defined as limiting or undermining the sharing of power, prestige, and privilege) in the community spilled over to the school system with the unforeseen consequence of depriving all children of quality education. Madison was unwilling or unable to recognize that its new racially mixed student/town population necessitated structural changes in the town and in the school. Closing ranks against diversity also syphoned off an economy that would have greatly improved the quality of life in Madison. The Indian population worked and purchased goods at nearby towns, draining off the potential for an expanding economic infrastructure in Madison.

The heroes of the Madison system are the students who graduate. Their tenacity is remarkable when you consider the grip that racism, teacher apathy, and budget parsimony has on this system. Their accomplishment is powerful evidence that education is important to this generation of students, belying the claim made by many that student apathy is the chief cause for the decline of American education. Targeting students as the culprits, obscures the reality that for many cities and towns, racism is the root cause of the decline in American education.

The classroom observations showed what is termed the "Pygmalion effect" described earlier in this book. It is not argued that teachers consciously have preconceived notions of Indian students' capabilities, but the fact is that classroom evaluations were evidence that the level of academic expectations they imparted for Indian students was lower than that for non-Indian. While better books and higher standards and course content would appreciably improve Madison's educational quality, it would not measurably effect the self-fulfilling prophesy that children of the Indian race were not destined to become scholars.

As principal of an Indian school that was a former Bureau of Indian Affairs school, I once informed teachers (who had worked in the BIA school previously) at the beginning of a term that the following year's contracts would be determined by the academic achievement of their students. They responded by notifying me that there were 103 "slow learners" and that the goal of having them all at their age-grade level was impossible. In May of the next year, miraculously, the average student improved 3.5 years in each subject on the SRA scores. The Pygmalion effect operates in mysterious ways.

Racism, as shown in the Madison study, does not necessarily have to be overt (although in the hiring practices, it was). Institutional racism hindered this school from developing a stable faculty because the high rate of turnover indicated that teachers came into the system and left with alarming frequency. The teachers available (and qualified) on the reservation were not hired, nor had the administration or the school board actively sought qualified Indian administrators. Half of the teaching staff were neophyte white teachers who stayed just long enough for the experience. Evidently, the alternative of hiring Indian teachers to provide potential faculty stability was not considered.

All students benefit from a multicultural faculty and curriculum. Minority students gain role models, while white students gain perceptions of different races that may in the future contribute significantly toward reducing institutional racism in this country. Would any child have been emotionally damaged by Indian posters on the wall? Would academic excellence be lessened by including Indian language for all children in the curriculum? Certainly, the opportunity for students to actually use Indian language daily was far greater than the opportunity to use French or Spanish. The inclusion of Indian history into social science is not revisionist history, but factual and contributes a broader base of knowledge that should be the goal of any school system.

Madison is a metaphor for the ills of public education. It will improve when and if the community understands that by depriving the Indians of educational equity, it is depriving its children as well. A national effort to improve educational quality must concomitantly concentrate on obliterating institutional racism in American communities. There is a valid argument in the assertion that race relations have improved in the past few decades. They have, but at a snail's pace and not commensurate with our national goal of producing quality education to compete in a global world.

We have two choices. We either improve our education system drastically and quickly to enable students of all races to work in a technologically advanced society, or we continue as we have been going and accept lower wages and a subsequent lower standard of living. Madison does not see this outcome because it sees itself as a breadbasket. But in truth, if the standard of living declines in the United States as that in other countries in Europe and Asia improves, there will also be a decline in Americans' ability to pay for food, which directly affects Madison.

Our global pre-eminence directly correlates to fashioning a meritorious society, that is, making it possible for every citizen to reach his or her full potential. Historians tell us this is what the founding fathers had in mind, but public policy tells us otherwise, even from the beginning. This country was founded on racism, which continues to exist, but in the past the economy provided a smoke screen against the reality. Today, that no longer exists as we navigate into a global economy. Reality and rhetoric are in sharp collision even in our sleepy little town of Madison, which is deteriorating under the yoke of institutional racism. The growth of Madison stagnated with the economy. This same effect can occur nationwide unless we recognize the power and strength of inclusion rather than exclusion.

The federal government has a vested interest in reversing this social cancer. The United States can only compete in a global twenty-first century if its citizens are well trained and well informed. In the past, institutional racism was a national embarrassment, but it did not interfere with America's ability to market our products overseas. Today it threatens our national economy to such an extent that we cannot compete with the newly emerging European common market or the Asian market. Our high-school graduates are technically and educationally inferior to those of Europe and Asia. American corporations are going overseas, not because of cheap labor as has been touted, but because it is easier and more efficient to integrate well-trained Asian and European high-school students into American corporate robotic, technological, and communications manufacturing. Countries such as Taiwan educate high-school students capable of understanding complex mathematical, chemical, and electronic machinery, and it is cheaper for American corporations to train them than to institute remedial programs to make American high-school students employable.[8] While we have been building better prisons, foreign countries have been building better schools.

It serves no purpose to wax nostalgic about the successes education enjoyed transforming European immigrants into the middle and upper middle class, because that model lacks one variable, race.[9] Classroom textbooks did not demean or gloss over the contributions of European culture to American society, nor did teachers perceive the children of immigrants as possessing inferior intelligence.

However, public education has hidden and/or summarily dismissed the historic legacy of having confiscated Indian lands and subsequent colonization of the American Indian and kidnapping the African American from Africa and subsequent enslavement in the United States. Textbooks have buried the stark reality that the wealth of this country has been largely derived from Indian lands and African American and Asian labor. Education has paid lip service to accepting the culturally different values of African Americans (who have not been integrated into all levels of American society) and American Indians (who justifiably resist being tossed into a racial food processor). Divorced from the historic past, the average American does not comprehend the contemporary conflicts rooted in the past. Ill-prepared to cope with the underlying causes of racial unrest and educational inequality, Americans turn to resolving guilt by "blaming the victim."

Even if the federal government began today with reversing the social cancer of institutional racism, it is doubtful that the effects would be felt inside of at least one generation. The solutions proposed are in direct opposition to those proposed by policy makers today. Recognize racism exists in every community and every institution, that the federal government has a vested interest in obliterating this social cancer, and use the tools at hand for at least an interim period between now and when the tenticles of institutional racism have been severed: educational vouchers.

The analysis of vouchers will be explored in the next chapter, but, simply put, we propose to convert entitlement funds into educational vouchers not exclusively to subsidize school systems, but to provide financial incentives for teachers whose students have achieved the national norm for their age-grade. In addition, in order to experiment before using a voucher system nationally, we propose using Indian education entitlement funds initially from Impact Aid and Title 4, part A, to provide incentives to teachers who would benefit if Indian students achieved age-grade level. Twenty percent of each voucher would go directly to teachers whose Indian students have achieved age-grade level, 80 percent to subsidize school systems. This proposition simply acknowledges that profit motive works wonders in this nation, and that you cannot change people's attitudes easily, but you can change educational outcomes.

In fact, we are arguing for a much more aggressive federal role in education, exactly the opposite of the social policy framers are recommending in 1995.

The Federal Role in Shaping
Local School Systems

Once in a while members of Congress should revisit a history class, because it appears these days they have contracted selective historic amnesia as they debate the appropriate federal role in public education. Some have taken the draconian position of eliminating the entire federal Department of Education positioning the nation's education systems exclusively under the state public education departments. Others argue for eliminating some programs within the Department of Education. A third voice argues for a more pro-active federal role in education until presented with compelling evidence of educational equity and excellence in every state.

Under close scruity, those in favor of shelving the U.S. Department of Education appear to have forgotten educational inequities presented in the Supreme Court decision *Brown vs. Topeka Board of Education*. The U.S. Department of Education was created to assure all American citizens an equal playing field through state education systems, and although far from perfect, it has a fundamental role to play in nationhood. Those who support shelving the U.S. Department of Education see merit in the traditional nineteenth-century model which established an arms-length federal involvement in state educational policies and standards. This federal policy satisfied both state and local Boards of Education at a time when the nation's schools reflected a local homogenous population, although no one can argue minorities received any where near equity under state mandates. Indian education, of course, remained under federal jurisdiction even after the Johnson O'Malley Act of 1934.

However, local homogeneity dissipated at the turn of this century as diverse immigration patterns emerged from southern and eastern Europe and Asia and South and Central America, transforming the nation's homogenous communities into a richly diverse racial and cultural heterogeneous nation. At this juncture, if the federal government had taken a directive position requiring all schools to implement full equity and/or excellence for all students, or if local public schools accommodated and included this new diversity as Dewey and other reformers proposed, our school systems would have been in far better shape than they are today. Either way, public policy would have made it far more difficult for institutional racism to become so deeply entrenched as it is today. But neither event occurred.

The absence of federal parameters assuring equity and excellence to all citizens allowed states to set their own parameters and tied the support of education systems to local taxes, with the inevitable result that poorer communities in any state had less than adequate school systems, while richer communities had better than average. By the 1950s, especially in the South, the national debate centered on whether the federal government had a constitutional responsibility to ensure educational equity for all citizens. Because school systems were largely supported by local property tax, if there was to be any federal role, it not only had to set some national standards, but it had to support these standards with massive federal funding. In other words, it had to offer a carrot with the stick.

It is not a coincidence that the civil rights movement was not as much about the right of all citizens to vote, or eat in any restaurant, as it was about the right to equality in education. Even after

Brown vs. Topeka, the federal government stayed within the boundaries of the nineteenth-century model, forging a reactive rather than a pro-active role to entice communities (through myriad subsidies) into support of educational equity. Well intentioned as these subsidies were, they did not permeate the root of inequality, institutional racism, in American communities. As we enter the twenty-first century, the education debate has gained momentum, polarized between those who want a minimal federal role in education and those who advocate a national stalwart leadership role overriding parochial local interests.

Neither argument recognizes two factors illustrated by the Madison study. Even with substantial federal subsidies, Madison was not held accountable for educational outcomes. In fact Madison received larger subsidies precisely because students were behind national and/or state age-grade norms. Had Madison been made accountable, that is, federal subsidies allocated and/or increased for successfully implementing excellence, doubtless the entrenched instutitional racism would have given way to pragmatic funding incentives.

No sovereign nation can afford to allow local parochial interests (illustrated by the Madison study) to supercede national interest. In a global, highly competitive economy it is national economic suicide to allow each local community to vote with its pocketbook. Again, using Madison as an example, cities and towns throughout the nation vote down tax increases for public education which will not change unless the federal government acts in the national interest to insist that each community meet federal standards for all citizens. Had federal standards mandated schools have an adequate school library, a science laboratory, language and computer classes, and a multicultural curriculum, it is unlikely that the Madison school system would have passed regional accreditation.

The federal government has within its power to change counterproductive behavioral patterns exemplified by institutional racism, not by legislation, but by information. Consider how the nation's attitudes have changed about drunk driving and smoking. The federal government began with allocating massive research funds to provide scientific evidence about the health hazards of smoking and drunk driving, followed by a media blitz to change American attitudes. Even half that concerted effort to document and disseminate the true cost of institutional racism on our economy would make a tremendous impact on education. Madison residents did not perceive the true cost of educational stagnation because no one told them concretely that mediocre education can and does affect the local economy.

Aside from the human cost of wasted lives, the federal government should document and disseminate the economic cost of institutional racism with the same zeal displayed in the smoking campaign. The public may be vaguely aware of the dollar cost of welfare, But it is not generally known what the actual cost is in terms of tax dollars lost to society when so many citizens are unemployed, unemployable, or institutionalized. American social ills have mushroomed to such an extent that annual state budgets propose heavier increases for programs or institutions to control deviant behavior, leaving a smaller percentage available for education. This cycle is shortsighted, untenable, and not in the best interest of the nation. Call it "propaganda" or call it "reality," but the average taxpaying citizen needs concrete, documented evidence connecting the practice of institutional racism to his or her standard of living. The federal government needs to intervene by making is unprofitable and untenable for communities to permit, sanction, or turn a blind eye on this social cancer, racism. A beginning would be strict enforcement of affirmative action in our economic, social, and educational institutions.

Hardly a day goes by when someone from either the federal or the state legislation does not assert that affirmative action is reverse discrimination and anathama to meritoriousness. Indeed, this hackneyed argument would carry weight if in fact we educated, hired, or promoted citizens equal to their capabilities in spite of race, income, or gender. If the anti-affirmative action forces succeed in wiping out affirmative action policies, the institution of education at all levels will experience an especially pernicious outcome on education.

Minorities can be just as well trained and talented as whites, and it is de facto colonialism to lock out minority professionals from educational systems, especially when the student body is minority. How in the world do we expect to persuade high-school minorities to stay in school when it is blatantly transparent that the few minorities who have graduated from college cannot work in the same capacity as their Anglo colleagues? Children believe what they see, not what is said.

The nineteenth-century model is inadequate to bring our education system into the twenty-first century. Federal intervention is critical to hurling parochial communities into meeting the needs of a global, technologically advanced society. Realistically, though, especially in the current political climate, it is political suicide to legislate federal programs en masse without supportive evidence of their efficacy. Indian education entitlement funds for public education systems offers the federal government an ideal learning laboratory, requiring no additional entitlement funds and only a small change in the legislative language. Transferring Indian education entitlement funds into a voucher system may not change entrenched instititional racism, but there is a good possibility that it can change educational outcomes. It is not proposed that vouchers be used for tribally controlled schools, because these schools already predict high student achievement.

11

Solutions for the Future: The Voucher Plan and Tribal Schools

America was founded on racism, and the institutions that evolved were formulated to institutionalize and justify racism. Colonial America used the institution of education as a means of detribalizing the Indian because in their Eurocentric perspective, tribal societies had little to offer the colonists and much to gain if they agreed to absorb institutions, religions and customs of the colonists. The experiment failed. Colonists resorted to genocide. Indians fought back. It is useful to remember that at no time did the colonists believe Indian culture was of any value, nor did they place any value on Indian lives. African Americans were valued solely for their labor, and indeed slavery was institutionalized throughout much of colonial America. The point is that education was one of the institutions that not only represented early colonial racism, but passed on generation after generation the concept of 'white supremacy,' not only because of what was taught, but, what is more important, what was not taught.

Generations followed, and education became a means to subjugate the American Indian and by withholding education from the African Americans, place them permanently into slavery. As waves of immigrants came after the Civil War and into the early part of the century, racism had been so completely internalized through the education system that few students up until only recently have ever been taught the real history of this country.

In this century, the United States became a world power, primarily because it had cornered the market for raw materials in third-world countries and had a rapidly industrialized labor force, mostly supplied by the new immigrants eager for work of any kind. But as third-world countries began to demand fairer prices for their raw materials, and as the children of immigrants were less complaisant about labor conditions, industry began using cheap labor from third-world countries, and slowly we have changed from an industrial society to a highly technological society. If there is a singular compelling force to change the internal structure of American institutional racism, it is the profit motive. That is, it is no longer profitable to have an undereducated society in a progressively highly technological world.

The third-world analogy should not escape the reader as he or she remembers that tribes toward the 1970s also began examining their own natural resources and the exploitation of corporate power, buttressed by the pervasive power of the Bureau of Indian Affairs. By the eighties, few tribes were willing to accept the old colonial model that had been so deeply entrenched over two hundred years. We demanded the right of our nationhood, meaning that our culture, our language, and our tribalism should be respected and accepted.

By this time, more than half of our children were being educated in public schools. The purpose of the Madison study was to demonstrate how completely institutional racism was entrenched in the school, because it was a mirror image of the Madison community. A more generalized view is that Madison is no different than thousands of other communities throughout the country. The same textbooks, teaching methodology, and Pygmalion effect operate in Los Angeles, New York, or Madison, wherever there are racial minorities or culturally diverse populations.

Institutional racism is pervasive, and we are now beginning to grasp the serious effect on this nation's role in a global economy. The United States has a vested interest in reversing more than two hundred years of institutional racism, because if we are to seriously compete in a post-technological global economy, we will need to educate all to the fullest potential. The federal government is in a doublebind. In a democracy, it is impossible to dictate by fiat, and yet the nation's standing as a world power is tied to dramatically changing the education system, which, in turn, is tied to the ethos of local communities where institutional racism is deeply entrenched and has been for hundreds of years. The federal government has a formidable task, made more difficult by the "blame the victim" mentality which currently exists in Congress. Even if that were not a fact, institutional racism and the concomitant role this social cancer plays in our nation's education system will not be reversed easily or quickly.

However, what can be reversed is education outcomes, not by fiat, but by selective use of a voucher system which has as its basic tenet an acceptance of the powerful role of a profit motive in American society.

The Voucher Plan

American Indians are the only group in this country over whom the federal government has held exclusive educational domain, partly because many treaties included education as a federal responsibility, and partly because it became the bedrock of the pacification and later assimilation policies. Even when Indians attend public schools, federal entitlements (covered earlier in this book) fund school systems through the Indian Education Act, Impact Aid, and the Johnson O'Malley Act. Federal entitlements are not in question here because they are part and parcel of the trusteeship relationship, but the fact is they have not lived up to the promise of providing equity or excellence for Indian students attending public schools. Madison illustrates that this school system provided annual reports of funding received and spent, but nowhere was there any information asked for or given as to what the funds bought in terms of equity and excellence. This leaves a sort of mystical belief that Madison, or any other school system will honor the legislative intent of these entitlements.

School systems do not teach children, teachers teach, and it is that individual teacher in the classroom who predicts student performance. The Pygmalion effect cannot be overemphasized, because even in substandard school systems, excellent teachers can override predictive student performance usually found in substandard systems. In the Madison school system, for example, there was a teacher who found a new way to teach math, and her students were truly remarkable in the speed and accuracy of complex mathematical computations. Also, it was evident that another teacher's Shakespeare students were thrilled with the language, drama, and poetry of the bard as they enacted scenes in the class. These two examples offer us insight into how individual teachers can light up a class even in subjects many students prefer to sleep through.

A voucher system that allocates a percentage of each student voucher to a teacher where that teacher can demonstrate, through end of the year testing, that the voucher student is at age-grade level can provide a powerful incentive for instilling teaching excellence and overriding conscious or subconscious predictions of student mediocrity.

Converting Indian education entitlement funds to public schools into vouchers (a percentage of which go directly to teachers) makes good sense for two reasons. One, by offering an incentive to teachers who are normally woefully underpaid for the work they do, it is highly likely that although their attitudes may not change, the profit motive can override stereotypic images of Indian students' ability to "master abstractions." Two, using Indian education vouchers, data collected over a period of three to five years can provide substantial concrete evidence that the nation's schools will function optimally if education entitlements are also converted into vouchers for each qualifying student by virtue of isolation, poverty, language, mental or physical handicap, or race. Indian students attend both rural and urban schools throughout the United States. Because they are scattered in all types of school and community settings, the data gathered from them can be easily and quickly generated and generalized to assess effectiveness of the same voucher plan on other minority students in the nation. They are an ideal working laboratory to substantiate the effects institutional racism has on the nations' schools. If this strategy works with the Indian student who has the highest dropout rate of any minority in the country and who is victimized by the Pygmalion effect as much as any other minority, it is highly probable it can succeed nationally. That kind of substantive evidence is exactly what is necessary to generalize vouchers nationwide.

This proposition recognizes that public misconceptions of racial intelligence are almost intransigent to change, but the impact in the classroom can be overcome by introducing a profit motive directed to teachers who in the final analysis can make a dramatic change in student achievement. In the past, entitlements have been directed exclusively to school systems. A more effective method of assuring educational parity for Indian students is to use the entitlement partially to reward teachers who bring and keep Indian students at their age-grade national norm. This strategy recognizes the power of self-prophesy, that if teachers think children can succeed, they succeed. To override negative predictions of student achievement, we add a powerful incentive: 20 percent of the Indian education voucher will go to teachers whose Indian students leave their grade at their age-grade level, measured by national norms administered by national testing instruments. In other words, rather than send the full entitlements to school systems who are removed from the teacher-student interaction, a percentage will be set aside to reward that teacher in the front line. Teachers, even those who are overtly racist, will work harder to ensure an Indian student's success overriding (and hopefully changing) their own deeply felt racial preconceptions if they are rewarded financially.

There are those who argue that we should get rid of teachers who even unwittingly are racist, but often even teachers are not aware of subconscious bias. A more pragmatic approach is to work with the Pygmalion effect, providing incentives to teachers (who are underpaid as a profession) to ensure positive student achievement. Of course, there are some pitfalls. Teachers may resort to winning "popularity contests," and school systems may have problems with unions because of the pay differential. On balance, systems can measure academic achievement with national testing norms minimizing rewarding popularity contests. Contemporary pedagogy recognizes the value of supporting teaching excellence with higher pay for master teachers or specialists, and this is simply an extension of that concept. Teaching unions may object, but since the Indian population is only about 1 percent of the school population and under federal trusteeship, unions may take a more relaxed position and wait to assess effectiveness.

This concept would benefit all minorities, but there is an additional benefit for Indian students. Until now, systems have tallied Indian students willy-nilly, some requiring affidavits of Indianness as required by law, but most, especially in cities away from Indian reservations, relying upon self-identification. In Fresno County, where the VISTA program has been involved in preparing Indian students to enter college, the Indian VISTA workers maintain that only one-fourth of the names given them by the school systems as Indian actually are Indian. It is not a matter of whether they are on tribal rolls (many California Indians are not federally recognized), it is a matter that they could not qualify by any definition, either Bureau of Indian Affairs, tribal, Indian organizations or the Office of Indian Education. Even though the new regulations insist upon qualifying the Indian enrollment, public schools have not complied. (At my own university, which relies upon self-identification, two hundred Indian students are listed as Indian, but only fifty know from what tribe they come).

Indian education entitlement funds are not a paltry sum. Set up as a congressional recognition that American Indian education is adjunct to treaty responsibilities, these funds have often provided substantial support for systems with a large Indian student population. In 1990 the Office of Indian Education allocated $73,620 million for the support of 351,641 Indian students. Only $3,451 million went to Indian-controlled schools with a student population of 4,781. Close to 51 million in entitlements went to public schools having 333,494 Indian students. One-third (109,280) of the Indian student population attend schools entitled to Impact Aid funds (Madison is an example because it is near the Indian reservation), which in 1990 was $243,690 million. 2,300 Indian students in vocational educational programs were supported through the Indian Vocational Education Program in the Department of Education to the tune of $12,622 million to 38 funded projects.

Apart from the entitlements, 1990 discretionary funding for Indian education amounted to $12,557 million, supporting 9,958 students; college fellowships $4,078 million, supported 128 Indian students. These fellowships are in reality a voucher system allocating money directly to the student and indirectly to colleges who reduce financial aid by the amount awarded through the fellowship. Not surprisingly, this program has had the most successful educational outcome of all the Indian education programs.

Vouchers are not a new idea. The federal government uses vouchers in delivering services to the poor for housing, nutrition, and health care. In the fifties, the federal government subsidized developers to build huge urban apartment complexes for low-cost housing for the poor. In the sixties and into the eighties, congressional hearings produced evidence that nefarious builders and bankers made huge profits from these well-intentioned federal programs. Little funds were available for maintenance, and within a decade these complexes became slums. Today we are tearing down these slums and rethinking our policies that the best and most effective means of providing housing to the poor is to provide the funds directly to the poor to buy their own apartments or house.

In the sixties, Doctor Hatch from South Carolina reported to Congress that there were Americans who had beriberi, which is a disease caused by nutritional deficiency, which is usually associated with third-world nations. Congress responded by enacting a commodities food program to provide surplus food to the poor. The trouble was, food commodities alone did not provide a well-balanced diet. Today, food stamps as the principal source of nutrition have replaced commodities, giving poor families purchasing power to buy a balanced diet.

These experiments are not without vocal detractors who argue that vouchers reduce individual initiative and increase dependency. But the research suggests that the most successful voucher programs target funds directly to recipients, bypassing distribution through institutions or corporations. Indian education entitlements can work in the same way, mixing the need for institutional support to school systems with vouchers directly going to teachers who succeed in bringing Indian students in their classroom to nationally normed age-grade level.

If 20 percent of the per capita entitlement funds went to individual teachers, there would be a dramatic and expeditious turnaround of Indian student achievement. Meticulous monitoring and evaluation administered on the state level is absolutely essential to the integrity of the program. This is one strategy that will not take long to assess the efficacy of because the merit payments will come at the end of the school year and after testing. Follow-up over a five-year period will either prove the Pygmalion effect works and consequently should be used nationwide, or it will prove it should be scrapped.

Vouchers will not eliminate institutional racism. But consider that even in Madison, where institutional racism is blatantly evident in the community and school, how many teachers would have worked harder to instill excellence within the Indian students if there had been a voucher system in place? Approximately 250 students in that system are Indian. Let us suppose that a voucher system was in place. The Madison system received approximately $1.2 million for construction of a new high school. Say that the balance of 200,000 was divided into 80 percent ($160,000) to the school system, and 20 percent ($40,000 or a little more than $2,000 per teacher in the Madison system) set aside for teacher vouchers. It is a reasonable assumption that the majority of teachers would use every creative method in existence to have Indian students in their classroom reach a national age-grade norm to receive a summer dividend. While the voucher may not change attitudes toward Indian students, it will change outcomes not only for the Indian students, but for all students. If there is money unused because teachers have not earned their dividend, a summer program could be initiated to improve teacher effectiveness.

Madison will not retreat from its position of institutional racism until the federal government produces substantial evidence of the cost to its standard of living. That will take time. In the meanwhile, the quickest, most efficient strategy to turn mediocre education into excellence is to use teacher vouchers and count on the resourcefulness inherent in the teaching profession. In any case, Indian Country cannot lose another generation of students to despair, dropouts, and counter-productive behavior. Something must be done, and quickly.

Most Indian students attend public schools, but a substantially growing number are now in tribal schools. Although the reservation in the Madison study opted not to develop a Kindergarten through twelfth-grade tribal school, many tribes choose this option for Indian children living on or near the reservation. These schools have been the focal point of a great deal of debate in Congress (remember the ABT report mentioned earlier). The next section is a discussion of these schools, because with or without a voucher system, tribal schools inherently believe Indian children can succeed academically and remain tribal Indians. The best chance an Indian child has to achieve academic excellence lies within the strengthening and growth of tribal schools.

Tribal Schools

The average American growing up in the cauldron of integrated education is bewildered by the recent emergence (and rapid expansion) of tribal schools. They may ask why, after decades of legal jousting, should anyone embrace an educational philosophy anathema to the civil rights movement and concomitantly, desegregation?

Philosophically, there is a reasonable level of assent to using tribal schools as remedies for Indian students with learning or behavioral problems. These they are able to justify as programs having short-term goals as differentiated from comprehensive public schools. In this age of budget deficits, some wonder what justifies allocating tax dollars to support Indian schools at a time when other minorities demand an end to de facto segregated schools?

The answer is simple: Indians are not treated politically as minorities, but as citizens of nations within a nation. This is not an abstract or temporary construct, but a constitutional reality guaranteed in the last century by treaties, and in this century by acts of Congress and Supreme Court decisions. In plain English, tribes have always had the legitimate authority to exercise dominion over the education of their young. That they have not until recently fully actualized this authority is due more to the constraints the Bureau of Indian Affairs has exercised by way of funding, facilities, and de facto colonialism. Even when the public accepts these fundamental principals, they ask why sovereign tribal nations should have a right to federal funds for Indian education. If in fact they are sovereign, does that not mean they should underwrite their own educational facilities? Again the answer is simple. For two centuries the federal government has exercised control over Indian education by virtue of treaty and de-facto colonialism, and the fact of the matter is, had they truly set out to educate Indian people rather than to use education as a substitute for pacification, tribes would be in a position to underwrite their own education systems. This is not naive, but based upon historical fact. The Cherokee Nation is a prime example of tribally supported education that would have been self-sufficient if left alone, but it was the federal government who sought and gained control over its education system, with the abysmal results outlined earlier in this book. In any case, there is no public or private college or primary or secondary school in this country that does not rely upon federal dollars for capitalization, student support, faculty, or programs.

The history of tribal demands for control over Indian education began in this century with the American Indian movement (AIM) in the 1960s. AIM viscerally and intellectually linked Indian control of Indian education with tribal sovereignty. The message struck a pan-Indian cord, uniting urban and reservation Indians to demand greater control over Indian education.

At first, Indian activists created alternative urban Indian schools. Edie Benton Binai, Clyde and Vernon Bellecourt in Minneapolis, and the Native American Education Program in Chicago were at the forefront of developing "Red School House" education programs. Initially, these urban programs were remedial. Some of these ceased to exist as funds began to dry up, but many exist today. The importance of these alternative programs cannot be overestimated, because tribes used them as models for experiments in the seventies. Later, the Red School House in Minneapolis and tribal schools such as Rough Rock on the Navajo reservation evolved into Kindergarten through twelfth-grade comprehensive schools. The larger tribes took greater risks in the chartering of tribal schools because the alternatives for many in these immense rural areas were the Bureau of Indian Affairs off-reservation boarding schools. But with the passage of the Indian Self-Determination Act in 1975, many of the smaller tribes seized the opportunity to develop tribal comprehensive primary and secondary tribal schools.

The models of Indian-controlled schools are as diverse as Indian Country. Some tribal schools were formerly Bureau of Indian Affairs off-reservation boarding schools. Some are public schools on the reservation, and there are several public schools under Indian control off the reservation. Some were initiated as cultural or linguistic tribal programs and eventually evolved into tribal schools.

The first BIA off-reservation boarding school to come under Indian control was the Pierre Indian School, renamed the Pierre Indian Learning Center. In 1975 tribes petitioned the Bureau of Indian Affairs to assume control and appointed a board member from each of the fifteen tribes in North and South Dakota and Nebraska. A number of other former BIA schools in New Mexico, Arizona, and Oklahoma followed suit.

One of the earliest reservation-based public schools was on the Omaha reservation in Macy, Nebraska. This school follows the requirements of Nebraska's public schools with the inclusion of Omaha language, art, history, and culture into the curriculum. Faculty and administrators are hired by the tribe and meet state credential standards. Both Indian and non-Indian students attend the school.

In Buffalo, New York, Lloyd Elm, one of the original board members of both the National Indian Education Association and the National Advisory Council on Indian Education (NACIE), directs a public school that integrates American Indian culture, language, and thought into a regular public school attended both by Indians and by non-Indians.[1] The annual NACIE report in 1988 highlighted this program as exemplary because it is recognized by the New York State Department of Education as a program meeting the state requirement for students knowing a language other than English and also as a research project validating using a holistic learning/teaching concept for Indian children.

Many of the urban Indian school programs/tribal schools concentrate as much on socially modifying counter-productive behavior as on acquiring or mastering academic skills. Prevention of drug and alcohol abuse and reduction in dropout rates play significant roles in achieving academic persistence. Examples of some prevention programs highlighted in the NACIE annual (1988) report are the City Camp Circle program of the United Indians of All Tribes Foundation in Seattle and the Minneapolis Public School program directed by Rosemary Christensen. Ojibwa uses a summer school program where Ojibwa language, cultural studies, health classes, nutrition, and family life are integrated into a holistic learning process.[2]

The word *holistic* is used by almost all Indian education programs/tribal schools, because unlike the public school systems, Indian Country does not separate education from culture, family, clan, or tribal life. It is a given in Indian education that the most efficient methodology for educating Indians is to treat students holistically and within a group process, as opposed to the competitive individualized methods used in the public system. There are exceptions, of course, but Indian educators have demonstrated remarkable success by using integrated interdisciplinary methods rather than single-subject discipline methods.[3]

During the embryonic stage the development of tribal schools, Indian parents were slow to accept tribal schools as a replacement for public or BIA schools. They did support tribal schools as a necessity for students who were having behavioral or learning problems, but were wary of their capability of delivering academic rigor for those without special needs. Like parents the world over, they wanted better opportunities for their young and questioned whether graduation from tribal schools would limit accessibility to higher education. Many were caught in a dilemma as they remembered attending the educationally inferior Indian schools operated by the Bureau of Indian Affairs. On the one hand, they wanted their children rooted in tribal language and culture, but on the other hand, they saw advantages in mastering biology and calculus. For many, it was an either/or proposition. But recent developments in tribal schools have allayed their fears. For instance, a tribal school on the Navajo reservation has recently sent five early admits to MIT.[4] Some tribes worked with major universities in the development both of alternative and of comprehensive K through twelve education system. The Zuni for instance, worked with Stanford University. This program is one of the by-products of the seventies when many Indians went to graduate school, formed a network after graduation, and sought help from each other. Hays Lewis and Linda Belarde on the Zuni reservation graduated from Harvard, as did Anne Medicine who is an assistant dean at Stanford University. Those graduates of the seventies are now in a position to work with graduates involved in tribal education programs, and this networking has created the potential for excellence in tribal schools.[5]

The ambition tribal schools have for Indian children is directly related to preparing the next generation to defend the interests of the tribe. To this end, many see the importance of acquiring mastery of the hard sciences. The Walapai use computers for language reinforcement in the Hualapai Bilingual Academic Excellence Program using Hypercard. An NIH project in more than twenty schools in New Mexico, serving Navajo and Pueblo elementary schools teaches curriculum on the prevention of chronic diseases and emphasizes nutrition, physical activity, self-esteem, peer pressure, and social influences through a native prospective.[6]

The evidence continues to mount that many tribal schools are more successful than adjacent public schools. Indian students at Harvard, Dartmouth, MIT, and Stanford are graduates of tribal schools, and they are well able to hold their own in the ivy League. There is a need for a rigorous comprehensive national study of tribal school effectiveness, because some have floundered while others flourished, and the contributing factors are not yet fully understood.

We do know that the tribal community colleges have had an impressive record of retaining and graduating Indian students, in spite of the remedial programs many must undergo before matriculation to a degree program. Nowhere has the linkage between tribal education and tribal development been more evident than the twenty-one tribal colleges on Indian reservations.

Tribal Colleges

Tribal colleges are not a new phenomenon. They originated in the last century but were closed down because of federal assimilation policies. In 1968 the tribal college movement surfaced again with federal funding of the Navajo community college.[7] In 1990 the Navajo's reported to Congress that "two NCC graduates are now medical doctors and both are caring for patients on the reservation, more have earned PhDs; two of whom are superintendents of school districts on the reservation; one has a successful business as a CPA; and there are many more who have finished bachelors and masters degrees working in tribal, state and federal agencies throughout the country."[8]

Paul Boyer headed up a two-year evaluation of tribal colleges, sponsored by the Carnegie Foundation for the Advancement of Teaching. In 1990 he submitted testimony before the Subcommittee on Postsecondary Education substantiating the remarkable success and progress of the Indian community colleges toward preparing Indian students for professional, vocational, and tribal careers. His findings reverse many of the allegations made about these colleges, namely, that they are not academically rigorous; they perpetuate isolationism and segregation; and they offer culturally based curriculum as a substitute for regular college academic programs providing a weak foundation for future employment.

> Tribal colleges offer a culture-based curriculum where traditional Indian culture is celebrated. . . . While much of white society identifies Indians with objects of the past—from tipis

to peace pipes—tribal colleges argue that traditional culture is more than artifacts. . . . But this emphasis on Native American culture should not be seen as an attempt to withdraw from contemporary society. Instead, an understanding of their past is seen as a way to build a strong future. For example, at least one study has shown that the Indian students who understand and accept their heritage have greater self-respect and are more likely to succeed academically.[9]

Tribal colleges are normally housed on tribal lands, but there are exceptions. The Native American Education Service (NAES) in Chicago began in the early seventies as the brainchild of the of Native American Center Board, Faith Smith, and Bob Dumont. They saw a need for a college degree designed for Indians working in the various social service agencies, mainly on the low-end para-professional level. Faith Smith became the head of NAES, and through persistence and vision she attracted first-rate faculty from surrounding colleges to work at low wages teaching at the NAES program. Classes began at 6:00 P.M. so people could come straight from work. This program has lasted beyond expectations. It now offers B.A.'s in many different fields, has satellite programs in Montana, and is accredited. Another urban Indian college, DQU, began ominously as an "Indian take-over" of surplus land in the early seventies at Davis, California. DQU began in turmoil, which plagued it for almost two decades. In the beginning, DQU had a modest curriculum plan, but through the years it has steadily upgraded its curriculum and is in the process of negotiating with the California State University system to become an American Indian feeder school to the system. These are only two colleges, but they are typical of the vision and originality of tribal colleges, not saddled by archaic rules and bureaucracy. They are designed to meet a need, and they do it with exceptional energy and dedication.

One of the earlier models of tribal colleges was so unique that students came from all over the country to attend. That was the Lummi Indian School of Aquaculture. The Lummi, a northwest fishing tribe, developed an extraordinary college program in marine biology and fish marketing to augment its sophisticated aquaculture program. It was a two year program designed strictly to acquire scientific knowledge of fish and marine life, so scant attention was paid to mastering Shakespeare 101, but it was designed by the Lummi for the Lummi. It more than served its purpose and has it evolved into an accredited community college serving many tribes in Washington.

Most Indians prefer not to leave the reservation, and most reservations have employment opportunities that require education. Heretofore, reservations have been obliged to hire non-Indians to fill many of the tribal professional and technical needs. Tribal colleges fill the gap between tribal manpower requirement and educational skills of tribal members. Boyer reported:

> Tribal colleges offer training for tribal needs. Because they are, in most cases, located on reservations and are run by tribal members, they know what skills their communities require. While courses range from certificates in welding at one college, a master's degree in elementary education, each college's curriculum is based on the understanding that most tribal members do not want to leave the reservation. . . . No non-Indian college or university can offer this direct link between the programs offered by the school and the needs of the reservation.[10]

In the past, tribal investment in higher education has not automatically led to strengthening of tribal development. There has been a poor fit between the needs of the tribe and the programs offered by state and private universities: "Tribal colleges sponsor development programs that directly benefit their reservation. Believing that their responsibilities are not limited to the students who enroll in their schools, all work to bring economic development and combat debilitating social ills."[11]

The funding of tribal colleges has been cost effective. Boyer mentioned that recent studies report between a 75 and 90 percent dropout rate of Indian students entering public colleges and universities, whereas the persistence rate (completion of a degree program) is extremely high in tribal colleges. There is a very good reason for this. Most graduates of tribal colleges are able to find work or continue with their education: A more recent survey of six tribal colleges found that one third of the graduates continued their education and that only 12 to 17 percent were unemployed. The survey noted that this contrasts with reservation unemployment rates that can soar to 85 percent.[12]

A number of the tribal colleges are now four-year institutions, and several offer master's degree programs. They are, from all evidence, the most highly sought and cherished educational institutions on the reservations. As the number of graduates increases, so will the number that will work for the tribe and tribal schools and contribute to the development and sovereignty of Indian Country.

In 1994, a bill was proposed in Congress to place tribal schools on the same federal funding level as the historically black colleges, which will give tribal schools funding stability as opposed to the annual or biannual funding they have been receiving. There is every hope that this bill will succeed and at long last tribal colleges can operate as other colleges with long-term plans for growth and continuity.

Perhaps the most telling reason for Americans to support tribal schools is that they work. Throughout this book we have examined the role institutional racism has played in the education of Indians. We no longer can allow this social cancer to affect Indian lives and tribal sovereignty. Using a voucher system for those Indian students attending public schools and support of tribal schools will make a substantial impact on achieving Indian Country's goals of self-sufficiency through academic excellence. There is no reason for children to have to choose between maintaining their culture and values and achieving academic excellence.

If one takes a broader perspective, the same forces that contributed to the abysmal academic record of Indian students affected all minority children in one way or another. In 1995 our national standing academically resembles more third-world countries that the highly technological countries with which we identify. For the first time in American history, institutional racism is no longer profitable if we are to compete in a global economy. The profit motive works in mysterious ways. In the next century, perhaps the profit motive will produce a vaccine for the institutional racism virus.

Epilogue: The White House Conference on Indian Education

I am often asked by well-meaning people "What do the Indians want?" How can you blame people for not knowing the dreams Indians have for the future, when the federal government, with hundreds of years of experience and a Library of Congress filled with federal Indian documents no one reads, is just as perplexed? The problem lies in succeeding generations perpetuating the historic amnesia of half truths, more to do with myth than the sheer reality of the confiscation of a continent. Even the nomenclature imbedded in history texts is specious, using such benign words as *discovery* when the appropriate term is *invasion* and *warfare* as a substitution for the more accurate term *genocide, resource and land development* instead of *property confiscation.* Indians know subconsciously or consciously that they are a colonized people, and they have much in common with tribal people the world over who have seen their lands confiscated. The justification used by the Dutch and English Africaans in South Africa, that they have "conquered the land" and are entitled to the fruits of their hard labor and industriousness, is the same logic imbedded in the American consciousness. Americans readily understand the reasoning behind international support of Mandela's demands and simultaneously dismiss Indian nationhood. Many Americans actually believe this land was sparsely settled centuries ago, when the fact is there were millions of natives, all with villages and lifestyles uniquely theirs. I often tell my students (to their amazement), "This may be your country, but it is my homeland." Even the complexity of Israeli-Palestinian conflicts are easier for them to grasp than that assertion.

What do the Indians want? Tribal sovereignty, the right to self-government free from state and federal colonialism, and the

181

understanding from American citizens that we are and have always been nations with a nation. We want Americans to finally learn the truth of their occupation of Indian lands. As a race of people, Indians have never been greedy. All that Indian Country is asking for is the right to control its own destiny upon what is left of current Indian property. And yes, Indian Country insists the bill must be paid by the federal government, by the citizens, as an infinitesimal payment for what was taken by force.

Tribal sovereignty is meaningless unless Indians educate those of the next generation to take their places in tribal affairs. Indian education has as its goal the eradication of centuries of colonial ethos imprinted on the minds and souls of Indian youth and to replace that model with one of pride, respect, and knowledge of Indian nationhood.

We have had convocations in the past as federal policy makers try to grapple with the seemingly unfathomable Indian obstinacy about being absorbed into the "Americanization" process, but the White House Commission on Indian Education appeared, at least on the surface, to justify some optimism that policy makers were willing to take direction from the Indians themselves.

Part of that optimism was due to the trust Indians had in Senator Inouye. Through persistent efforts on the part of Senator Inouye, chairman of the Senate Select Committee on Indian Affairs, and support from Committee Member Senator De Concini, P.L. 111–297 was passed in 1988. This legislation (coupled with subsequent amendments) authorized the planning, staffing, funding, and convening of 160 nationally known Indian educators and leaders to the White House Conference on Indian Education.

Senator Inouye, a staunch supporter of Indian Self-determination, follows in the footsteps of John Collier and Senator Abourezk in championing tribal sovereignty. His accomplishments have been formidable, since he became chairman of the committee. Interestingly, he joined the committee because as he said, "When I came to the Senate I found no one wanted to serve on this committee." The Great Spirit works in mysterious ways.

Within a brief time after joining the committee, Senator Inouye became aggravated over the self-serving grip the Bureau of Indian Affairs had on the federal political system. He reasoned that a substantial contributing factor was the annual, often ad hoc, appropriations process, allowing bureau officials to wield considerable power in the distribution of program funds to the tribes. He and other members of the committee sought a means by which Congress could forge a long-term blueprint for Indian education, reasoning administratively at least that Indian education should be less vulnerable to the vagaries of congressional elections. He argued that such a long-term planning process ought to be developed by Indians as a basis for future legislation, and not from Indians working in Washington, D.C., but from Indians working in the field of education throughout the country. Indian Country owes a debt of gratitude to this courageous senator.

The Pre-Planning Process

The legislative language for the White House conference predetermined the number of delegates selected (160). The number of state delegations was proportionate to the Indian population within the state. California had the largest delegation, and a number of eastern states with small Indian populations were allocated a fraction of a person.

It was impressive that careful attention was paid to include Indian populations that the Washington Indian policy oligarchy had routinely by-passed for decades, namely small tribes, federally unrecognized tribes, and urban Indian communities. This was particularly momentous for the Indians in California.

Historically, California has had a Machiavellian relationship with its Indian population. Unlike other states that (albeit reluctantly) acknowledged federal supremacy over Indian relations, California actually succeeded in preventing ratification of eighteen treaties in 1853, leaving the indigenous population in a legal quagmire which continues to this day.[1]

As a legal remedy for not setting aside reserved lands for California Indians, presidential executive orders were issued establishing 117 reservations and/or rancherias at the turn of this century. Currently, there are approximately 89 reservations/rancherias, most with a small land base and population.[2] Left with only a fraction of their original landholdings and population, many California tribes were again victimized by being the first to experience termination during the the 1950s. Withdrawal of federal recognition and protection left many California tribes, once again, landless. To compensate the Indians of California for the land confiscated in the last century, in the 1960s the Indians Claims Court awarded them a paltry 47 cents an acre. Adding to this indignity, Congress passed P.L. 280 which gave California considerable authority over the remaining unterminated Indian reservations.

Ironically, even though the indigenous population is exceedingly small, California's Indian population is the largest in the country, because ninety percent of the Indians come from tribes other than the state. This was the aftermath of the "relocation" policies of the fifties when large masses of rural Indians were placed within California's urban centers for employment and vocational education opportunities. It is not unusual, for instance, to find tribally enrolled second- and third-generation Navajos who were born and raised in California. While both of these populations have much in common, there are considerable differences as well, meaning that the selected California delegates had to be sensitive to those common concerns, and also to the needs of the indigenous rural and the diverse urban Indian population. Other states, of course, have the same reservation and urban mix, but in these the urban Indian generally comes either from that state or from those adjacent to it, making the populations more homogeneous than those in California.

The federal government has been exceedingly cavalier about pursuing trust responsibilities and protection to California's urban, tribal, and terminated Indians and often pitted the larger and more powerful western tribes against California Indians when tribal support was sought for budget decisions in Washington, D.C. It was a welcome change to find that the legislative language mandated that selection of delegates would include the full participation of the nation's diverse Indian population. The House, the Senate, and the White House were each to select one-third of the delegates from each of four categories:

1. Individuals who are currently active educators on Indian reservations;

2. Educators selected from urban areas with large concentrations of Indians;

3. Individuals who are Federal and tribal government officials; and

4. Individuals who are Indians, including members of Indian tribes that are not recognized by the federal government.

The federal register of November 2, 1990, carried a notice "Call for Nominations to the Advisory Committee for the White House Conference on Indian Education," and stated as the purpose to

1. Explore the feasibility of establishing an independent Board

of Indian Education that would assume responsibility for all existing Federal programs relating to the education of Indians; and

2. Develop recommendations for the improvement of education programs to make the programs more relevant to the needs of Indians.

At the 1990 National Indian Education Conference, Indians were asked to present papers on issues they wanted discussed at the perspective White House conference in 1992. The White House Task Force synthesized thirty-five topics for discussion garnered from the National Indian Education Association (NIEA) conference and statewide meetings with tribal leaders. Obviously, that was too large an agenda for a two-day conference, but it was a beginning for every state White House Steering Committee to work with local and regional Indian education organizations.

During spring and summer 1991, steering committees were formed in each state, and they in turn convened local and regional Indian education tribal agencies or organizations. In California, for instance, contacts were made in June, and each regional office met to discuss the thirty-five recommendations as well as President Bush's Education 2000 goals. The task was to examine the suggested topics, add any of our own, and organize them within the Bush administration's Education 2000 categories. Not easy.

President Bush's national educational goals were:

1. By the year 2000, all children in America will start school ready to learn.

2. By the year 2000, the high school graduation rate will increase to at least 90 percent.

3. By the year 2000, American students will leave grades four, eight and twelve having demonstrated competency in challenging subject matter including English, mathematics, science, history and geography; and every school in America will ensure that all students learn to use their minds well, so they may be prepared for responsible citizenship, further learning and productive employment in our modern economy.

4. By the year 2000, U.S. students will be first in the world in science and mathematics achievement.

5. By the year 2000, every adult American will be literate and will possess the knowledge and skills necessary to compete in a global economy and exercise the rights and responsibilities of citizenship.

6. By the year 2000, every school in America will be free of drugs and violence and will offer a disciplined environment conducive to learning.

No one can quarrel with these goals. However, as the delegates gleaned through the booklet distributed by the administration, questions were raised about the genuine commitment to educational excellence.

"America 2000—An Education Strategy." In the "some questions and answers" section *"How much will the America 2000 plan cost" the statement was made . . . State and local governments provide more than 90 percent of all education funding . . . a responsibility both the President and the Governors have concluded should not be altered. But America 2000 is not expected to raise state or local spending."* An air of cynicism prevailed during our deliberations, because anyone in the field of education knows that local governments are strained to their limit to provide even adequate education, and it is only the federal government who can provide leadership, incentive, and funds to bring our nation's schools to levels of excellence.

President Bush's goals, while valid for education in general, did not address the unique needs of American Indian tribes as separate and sovereign nations. Nor was there recognition of the barrier institutional racism in American communities places on excellence in teaching and learning. In fact, the Bush administration wanted Indian educators to address the aforementioned goals, with perhaps a slight flavor of Indian. Indian educators chose to set their own agenda and include the White House agenda where suitable. As the expression goes, "We've come a long way, baby."

The process of determining Indian education goals as a part of and apart from the White House goals was almost excruciating. After the preliminary local meetings, the statewide California delegates met in Sacramento, voted, agreed upon the issues, and nominated delegates to the White House conference. We sat back and waited.

However, the White House did not approve statewide nominated delegates until two weeks before the conference, giving very little time to make arrangements. Because of the information they required (a resume, picture, and social security number), many delegates assumed that an FBI check was done before delegates were approved.

The Final Task Force Categories Organized in Washington, D.C.

The task force synthesized the state resolutions into eleven topics. These were

1. Governance of Indian Education/Independent Board of Education

2. Well-Being of Indian Communities and Delivery of Services

3. Literacy, Student Academic Achievement, and High-School Graduation

4. Safe, Alcohol/Drug-Free Schools

5. Exceptional Education

6. Readiness for School

7. Native Languages and Culture

8. Structure for Schools

9. Higher Education

10. Native, Nonnative School Personnel

11. Adult Education and Lifelong Learning; Parental, Community, and Tribal Partnerships.

The White House Conference

Each of these topics addressed specific issues, and yet as each group presented proposed resolutions, they had an easily discernible commonalty. All of them stated a need to affirm the federal government to tribal government relationship,[3] an emphasis on accurate data, and the flow of information to the Indian communities,[4] control of funding, monitoring and evaluation to insure educational outcomes tied to additional funding especially in the public sector,[5] and high expectations for achievement and defining the institution of education holistically. This last point was especially pertinent to delegates who viewed education as integral to economic development, health, and social and traditional tribal institutions. Federal agencies treat each of these functions separately. However, tribal governments have consistently argued that these are like spokes in a wheel. Education is health, social services and economic development and should be funded and administered to integrate all of these programs into one holistic tribal plan for self-sufficiency.

Monitoring the state use of funds to public districts has also been a consistent thread in various Indian education studies, dating as far back as the sixties. State compliance has been lax. The delegates strongly urged Congress to put teeth into the monitoring, evaluating, and data-gathering regulations, by mandating that each state hire Indian professionals to carry out this responsibility. The key word used by the delegates was *outcomes,* that is, correlating Indian student achievement with annual public-school funding. Institutionally, the delegates wanted the federal government to require states to form an Indian Board of Education to receive and distribute funds to public schools, which, it was felt, would make public schools accountable for the funding they receive. The discussion that follows centers on resolutions stirring the most controversy and those receiving unanimous votes on the first round.

Topic 1: Governance of Indian Education Independent Board of Education

This topic is an example of the chasm between government policy makers and those at the local tribal/urban Indian level. In Washington, the creation of a centralized Indian Board of Education was a logical point of departure from the fragmented policy of old. Because Indian education funds come from many different agencies (other than the traditional Bureau of Indian Affairs and the Office of Indian Education) it was felt that funneling these funds into a super agency would bring about better monitoring and more effective planning and avoid duplication and dilution of scarce educational dollars.[6] Those opposed to this legislation felt that this super agency had the potential of being dominated by the largest tribes, while the smaller ones would be left without funding. For them, a super agency was too much power in the hands of too few people. The California delegation both at the state and at the national levels voted against an independent education board. They were not alone. Other state delegations had arrived at the same conclusion. But everyone was equally concerned that Indian education funds be monitored by Indians, and in this vein, proposed that each state create an Indian Board of Education as the receiver, disburser, and evaluator of Indian education funds. This compromise proposed by those opposed to a national board also turned into a heated debate. Tribes, exercising sovereignty, wanted all education funds to be funneled to them. Through tribal departments of education, funds could then flow to public school systems and/or colleges for the benefit of their tribal members. This raised a red flag to those states whose Indian populations predominantly came from tribes outside the state. In the end, a compromise was reached. Bureau of Indian Affairs funding and those funds directed toward tribal development should go directly to the tribes, while Office of Indian Education funds and those of other funding programs benefiting Indians living off the reservation (vocational, Indian health scholarships, etc.) would flow into an existing Office of Indian Education or a newly created State Indian Board of Education.

The resolutions proposed by the spokesperson for topic 2, Well-being of Indian Communities and Delivery of Services; topic 3, Literacy, Student Academic Achievement and High-School Graduation; topic 4, Safe Alcohol/Drug-Free Schools; topic 5, Exceptional Education; and topic 6, Readiness for School were passed unanimously, with minimal discussion. A paramount concern expressed with the passage of these resolutions was inclusion of appropriations to enable full funding of support services for families of students, including physical and mental health and academic, counseling and day care.

At least half of the delegates had experienced extreme negative expectations in the school systems they attended and expressed a strong plea that the next generation would not have to live through the same emotional battering: "Native students must be encouraged to reach high goals and receive instruction and academic counseling. This is from early childhood to higher education."

Topic 7: Native Languages and Culture

The resolutions proposed by the spokesperson for this topic and voted upon without dissension probably will have the most resistance by individual state education agencies and universities. From the prospective of Indian Country, these resolutions represent significant changes in the ways public schools and colleges have educated the vast majority of Indian people and, what is more important, provide for the future of Indian Country into the twenty-first century. The resolution proposed the federal government to amend Senate Bill 2044 to provide for

A. Inclusion of "Language, Literacy and Culture" in the Title; and use of the terminology "Language/Culture throughout the Act.

B. Development of curricula for Language/Culture, together with appropriation levels which enable the restoration of lost languages; and an overall appropriation of $200 million for language, literacy and culture including model programs.

C. Development of language literacy and culture certification standards by tribal governments, recognition of such certification by SEEA's and accrediting institutions; and appropriation levels which enable full implementation of the standards.

D. Establishment of course credit for Native Language classes at institutions of higher education, by students who demonstrate literacy and proficiency in Native languages.

E. Inclusion of American Indian/Alaska Native history and culture as a requirement for teacher certification of all teachers.

F. Availability of appropriated funds to Indian/Alaska Native tribes and organizations including urban and rural Indian organizations, for Indian/Alaska Native language and culture.

G. Allow American Indians and Alaska Natives to assume total responsibility for their education programs.

H. Require state and local education agencies that receive federal funds to include American Indians and Alaska Native language, culture and history into core curriculum.

The delegates also felt very strongly that tribal schools would continually be behind unless funding is sharply increased for technology (computers, satellites, informational networks), libraries and well-trained Indian educators.[7]

Topic 9: Higher Education

The emphasis on making higher education accessible (and affordable) to Indians as a cornerstone of tribal development was evident in the content of the resolutions proposed. By far, resolutions centered upon two factors; networking Indian students so that upon graduation they would return to work for Indian Country and the support and development of tribal colleges. Increasingly, tribal colleges have emerged as the cornerstone of tribal sovereignty. They, above all institutions higher education, have dovetailed education to meet employment demands on the reservations. Some of them are no longer two-year colleges, but offer B.A.s and M.A.s and prepare students to enter professional studies at universities. They are now poised for a more directive role in the training of potential teachers, research and curriculum development. One of the resolutions requested that federal legislation "provide *technical assistance to tribal governments* in the formation of tribal education agencies and policies, and the development of articulated agreements between states and tribes toward resolving cross-jurisdictional issues."

To drive home their point, the delegates requested that legislation be enacted "to provide *direct financial support to tribal governments* for establishing tribal departments of education, development of educational blueprints and tribal codes and/or ordinances governing education."

Almost half of the resolutions centered on tribal schools at the primary, secondary, and college levels. The development of these schools requires not only capital, long-range funding for curriculum development, advanced technology, and libraries but also trained Indian personnel. The delegates unanimously voted to have the federal Indian education policy require "consideration for a sequence of funding reflecting realistic planning, pilot, phase-in, and full program funding progression and that the White House Conference mandate an increase in the number of Native Americans recruited, trained, and hired into the teaching profession."

Rather than re-invent the wheel as so often happens in Indian education, the conference voted to establish a National Study Group on Pedagogy in Indian Education so that Indian educators would form a national information network and share information about the efficacy of different teaching strategies in all grades, including college.

The conference focused a good deal on the development, improvement, and stability of tribal community colleges. There was virtually no dissension in the resolutions for congressional action

to amend the Tribally Controlled College Act to increase funding
for graduate studies at these colleges, funding for the construction
of school facilities (many are operating out of mobile homes), funding for technical assistance to increase the efficacy of these colleges,
and to support non-Indian students attending these tribal colleges.

Indian Country has long sought an American Indian university. An important resolution was for the president and Congress to
"support the American Indian Higher Education Consortium efforts
to develop the consortium's distance learning capabilities which
have the potential to establish an American Indian University
Network."

The establishment of an American Indian university raises
many questions. Some delegates, particularly those representing
tribes having tribal colleges, argued that an Indian university ought
to rise organically from an existing Indian college. The remarkable
success tribal colleges have had on tribal development argues for
greater expansion into a comprehensive university. Others felt that
a comprehensive university offering professional degrees in law and
medicine and doctoral programs ought to be near a major university. Access to and support from public and private existing medical
centers, law libraries, graduate programs, and faculty would go a
long way to bringing an American Indian university into a reality.
At this time, tribal colleges are not receiving full appropriations
necessary for them to function optimally, so the matter was tabled
until such time as these colleges receive adequate appropriations
fearing that any change of direction would siphon off precious funds
needed for tribal colleges.[7]

An interesting analogy was made when the delegates proposed
that the president and Congress support tribal colleges at least to
the level shown for the historically black colleges:

> Therefore, be it resolved, that the White House Conference
> recommends that the President of the United States issue an
> Executive Order for the Tribally Controlled Community Col-
> leges (TCC), such that all cabinet level departments of the
> federal government identify resources and implement con-
> tracts with Tribally Controlled Community Colleges to perform
> research and advance study; to achieve equity with President
> Reagan's Executive Order for Historically Black Colleges and
> University.

At this writing, legislation has been presented to Congress to
appropriate financial support for the Indian colleges at the same

level as that of the historically black colleges, and although not certain, it is likely it will pass into law.

More than one hundred resolutions were passed at the White House conference. If half of them are legislatively enacted, we will make spectacular inroads into achieving academic excellence in the primary, secondary, and university levels. Indian Country is fired up to achieve educational equity with non-Indians. Congresses come and go, and there is no way of knowing whether they will use these resolutions as a blueprint for future legislation. One might be excused for a certain level of pessimism in light of recent federal congressional proposals to eliminate or minimize the federal role in education. However, there are and always will be visionaries in Congress and the White House who acknowledge Indian self-determination as honorable, just, and contemporary.

We began this book with a history of federal-Indian policy and asserted throughout the right of the Indian race to determine its own destiny. The twenty-first century is upon us. We are at the crossroads of determining whether America will honor cultural diversity and draw upon the strength this diversity brings to the social fiber of this country, or whether in fear of the unknown, withdraw into a monolithic and frighteningly rigid society. Anyone who has ever spent any time in the woods or pristine meadows untouched by the plow knows the value and beauty of diversity. In nature, diversity allows each plant or tree to grow to its fullest potential. Walking through these patches is a visual feast. I do not think it is possible for anyone to relish the gift of nature's diversity and reject the richness of cultural diversity. Choose.

NOTES

Introduction

1. Alexander Astin, *Minorities in Higher Education* (Jossey Bass Publ., 1982).

2. Terrel Bell, *A Nation at Risk* (National Commission on Excellence in Education, May 5, 1983).

3. Michael Katz, *Class, Bureaucracy and Schools* (Praeger Publ., 1971).

4. Robert Rosenthal, *Pygmalion in the Classroom* (Holt, Rinehart & Winston, 1968).

5. *Indian Country* is a legal term which refers to lands currently held in trust by the federal government for the benefit and use of Indian nations or lands once held in trust for tribes where treaty rights, such as those pertaining to fishing and water, have not been extinguished by congressional legislation.

6. An example is John Quincy Adams who remarked in 1802: "There are moralists who have questioned the right of Europeans to intrude upon the possessions of aborigines in any case and under any limitations whatsoever. But have they maturely considered the whole subject? . . . Shall the lordly savage . . . forbid the oaks of the forest to fall before the ax of industry and rise again transformed into the habitations of ease and elegance? Should he doom an immense region of the globe to perpetual desolation, and to hear the howlings of the tiger and wolf silence forever the voice of human gladness?" (quoted in U.S. Interior Department, Office of Indian Affairs, *Report on Indian Affairs . . . for . . . 1867*, p. 144).

7. For a well-documented analysis of Vittoria's *Doctrine of Discovery* and Vattel's response, see S. Lyman Tyler's English translation of both philosophers in Tyler, *Concerning the Indians Lately Discovered* (University of Utah, 1980).

8. Annual Address before Congress, President Jackson, 1830, U.S. Government Documents.

9. Jackson's cavalier attitude toward the U.S. Supreme Court left a legacy still felt in the twentieth century. He was persuaded by influential elites from Tennessee and Georgia to uphold states rights over federal supremacy and in so doing, he opened the door to the Southern states passing legislation that violated the Constitution. This was one of the factors contributing to the Civil War and the later civil rights movement.

10. Van Every, *The Disinherited* (1975).

11. Ibid.

12. Senator Frelinguysen, *Register of Debates in Congress,* 1830.

13. Ibid.

14. An excellent analysis of corporate exploitation of Indian resources can be found in Al Gedicks, *The New Resource Wars* (Boston: South End Press, 1993).

15. On August 10, 1981, the Senate committee held meetings regarding an oil theft from the Blackfoot reservation, which involved oil trucks leaving the reservation without the requisite weigh-in and stamp supplied by the Bureau of Indian Affairs to keep tighter controls over the energy corporations apparently with little success.

16. Kerr McGee claims that the Navajo deaths are due to an unhealthy diet and lifestyle. However, unlike the Silkwood case, the Bureau of Indian Affairs has base-line data because they have kept health records over a century in each of the small communities of the Navajo reservation and report lung cancer as rare up until the time of uranium mining on the reservation. To add to the Navajo distress, there has been an unexplained dramatic increase in the number of abnormal births and severely handicapped babies since the onset of uranium mining.

17. The Bureau of Indian Affairs as trustee has fiduciary responsibilities and is mandated to oversee the leasing contracts of tribal timber to private corporations.

18. American Indian Policy Review Commission, U.S. Government Documents, 1978.

19. Ibid.

20. *Hearings before the Senate Select Committee on Indian Affairs,* U.S. Government Documents, 1982.

21. Peter Matthiessen, *Indian Country,* 305.

22. These handouts were given to students. One reached the tribal office. The tribe acted immediately and lodged a strong protest much to the surprise of the officials of the Ferndale school system. They expressed surprise that the Indians took offense.

23. The vocal outrage expressed by Indians coast to coast persuaded retailers to refuse to sell this game.

24. Ross Swimmer, as head of the Bureau of Indian Affairs, opposed almost all of the legislation proposed by Indian Country including the Indian Child Welfare Act. He was a banker from Oklahoma and when the Cherokees were first permitted to vote for their tribal council in 1979, he ran for office and became the first principal chief of the Cherokees duly elected since the end of the last century.

25. *Report on the Board of Indian Commissioners,* 1883, 69–70.

26. Ibid.

Chapter 1

1. Benjamin Franklin, *Two Tracts.*

2. An comprehensive history of the Cherokee education system was written by Robert Howard Skelton as his dissertation in 1970: *A History of the Educational System of the Cherokee Nation, 1801–1910* (Ann Arbor: UMI).

3. Curtis Jackson and Marcia Galli, *A History of the Bureau of Indian Affairs and Its Activities among Indians* (San Francisco: 1977. R&E Publishing Co,.) 71.

4. *Hearings before the Subcommittee on Indian Education of the Committee on Labor and Public Welfare,* 1969, U.S. Government Documents.

5. Samuel Bowles and Herbert Gintis, *Schooling in Capitalist America,* (New York: Basic Books, 1976), 123.

6. Margaret Szasz, *Education and the American Indian* (Albuquerque: University of New Mexico Press, 1974), 17.

7. John Dewey, *Experience and Education* (New York: Macmillan, 1938), 48–50.

8. Lewis Meriam, *The Problem of Indian Administration* (Baltimore: Johns Hopkins Press, 1928), 83

9. Ibid., 403.

10. Ibid., 400.

11. NAACP Legal Defense and Educational Fund, Inc., and the Center for Law and Education, *An Even Chance* (Harvard University, 1971), 67.

12. Ibid., 27–40.

13. Ibid., 11–26.

14. Ibid.

15. Ibid.

16. Ibid.

17. Ibid., 5–10.

18. Ibid., 60.

19. James S. Coleman, *Equality of Educational Opportunity* (Washington D.C.: U.S. Government Printing Office, 1966), 275.

20. Alphonse D. Selinger, *The American Indian High School Drop-Out: The Magnitude of the Problem* (Indian Education, 1969), *Hearings before the Subcommittee on Indian Education of the Committee on Labor and Public Welfare*, U.S. Senate, 1015–1313.

21. Margaret Szasz, *Education and the American Indian* (Albuquerque: University of New Mexico Press, 1974), 152–53.

22. *An Even Chance*, 11–23.

Chapter 2

1. Tribal schools are generally found on rural Indian reservations. The exceptions fall into the category of formerly operated Bureau of Indian Affairs schools deliberately built away from Indian reservations or public schools under Indian control.

2. Judith S. Kleinfeld, et al., *Alaska's Small Rural High Schools: Are They Working?* (Fairbanks: Alaska University, Center for Cross-Cultural Studies, Institute of Social and Economic Research, 1985).

3. Ibid.

4. Judy T. Bates, "Portrait of a Successful Rural Alternative School," *Rural Educator* 5 (Spring 1993): 14 n. 3, 20–24.

5. Ibid.

6. "Discrimination and Differential Treatment: The Risk to Children," in *Barriers to Excellence: Our Children at Risk*. National Coalition of Advocates for Students, January 1985. 1–31.

7. Ibid.

8. Ibid.

9. They have yet to hold public schools accountable for the annual Indian education entitlement funds and/or low achievement of Indian students attending these schools.

10. In point of fact, the funds tribal control schools receive are taken to a large degree from the education budget of the Bureau of Indian Affairs and Indian education entitlements in the Department of Education. These agencies had more than an ax to grind; they had budget cuts they wanted restored to their domain.

11. Barriers to Education. *Our Children at Risk,* 1–31.

Chapter 3

1. ABT Associates, An Evaluation of Indian Controlled Schools, Contract #300-84-0267, September 6, 1985.

2. Ibid.

3. Ibid.

4. Ibid.

5. Ibid.

6. Ibid.

7. Ibid.

8. Ibid.

9. Ibid.

10. Ibid.

11. Ibid.

12. There were a number of changes in the Indian Education Act Title 5 when it was re-authorized in 1988, but since the study was done under the original provisions, Title 4 will be used throughout.

13. Logically, if it is easier to distinguish whether public schools are using federal Indian education entitlement funds to supplement rather than supplant operating costs, why did not ABT pursue this line of inquiry? This has been the continual complaint of Indian people, and it would have helped shed some light on why Indian Country has been so disillusioned with the public school. It would have helped the research project to compare how the Indian education entitlement funds are used by the public schools with those used by ICS.

14. ABT Associates, An Evaluation of Indian-Controlled Schools, Contract #300-84-0267, September 6, 1985.

15. Tribal cultures differ markedly, but the values appear to be consistent throughout; affiliation and responsibility to the tribe; personal responsibility; self-control; knowledge and understanding of tribal culture, including the language, history, religion, arts, dance, and music.

16. ABT Associates, An Evaluation of Indian-Controlled Schools.

17. Ibid.

18. Ibid.

19. Ibid. ABT felt constraint from unyielding Department of Education guidelines. It makes one question whether the Department of Education was truly interested in an assessment or whether it wanted a report to vindicate its position that the Self-Determination Act should be amended to force tribal schools to adapt to federal or state regulations.

20. ABT Associates, An Evaluation of Indian-Controlled Schools.

21. ABT admitted it could not ideally "match" tribal schools with local or neighboring BIA or public schools, but argued it was as good a match as possible.

22. ABT Associates, An Evaluation of Indian-Controlled Schools.

23. The language of the report is confusing. Put it another way and it reads: out of one hundred Indian students attending public school, forty-four had some Indian language capability. Out of one hundred Indian students attending tribal schools, fifty-five spoke their tribal language. Out of 100 students attending BIA schools, thirty-five spoke their language.

24. These differences are so marked that under circumstances (the intransigence of the Department of Education research guidelines) most evaluators would have redesigned the whole project.

25. Ibid.

26. Whenever public or BIA schools receive federal money, they are obligated to submit annual reports and permit their schools to be evaluated by the federal government. The Self-Determination Act places the responsibility of accountability with the tribe and holds the federal government at arms' length.

27. Tribes raised the question of whether quality control or control was the focal point of the Department of Education and Bureau of Indian Affairs' request for assessment. In any case, they could not mandate this evaluation (under the Self-Determination Act), and a number of schools declined to be part of the study.

28. The Department of Education has shown little if any concern about the quality of education Indian children receive in public and BIA schools even though the drop-out and under-achievement rates soar. They have yet to hold these schools accountable even though many receive annual Indian education entitlement funds.

29. National Coalition of Advocates for Students, *Barriers to Excellence: Our Children at Risk*, 1–31.

Chapter 4

1. It is worth noting here that James Coleman and others in their massive report *Equality of Educational Opportunity*, relied exclusively on statistical data, probably because of the sheer massive survey of 570,000 students and 10,000 teachers and principals in over 4,000 schools in the United States. When the survey tried to get at the sociological aspects of the learning variance between white and black, Puerto Rican, American Indian, Chicano and Asian students, statistical methods were used. See James Coleman et al. (Washington D.C.: U.S. Government Printing Office, 1966).

Samuel Bowles and Herbert Gintis, *Schooling in Capitalistic America* (New York: Basic Books, 1976), among others, criticized this approach, examined the internal expectations of education systems, and found that the educational output for minorities correlated to the expectations of school systems, teachers, curriculum planners, and textbook authors.

There were a number of educators after the Coleman report was published that argued for examining schools from within rather than chiefly relying upon data for information, because statistical analysis does not lend itself to understanding the hidden messages systems give to children. Yet, even after years of debate on the subject, the Department of Education and ABT used the survey-statistical method exclusively for their study. No one, either in the Coleman report or in the ABT study observed a class.

2. G. Ladson-Billings, *The Dreamkeepers* (San Francisco: Jossey Bass, 1994); E. E. Garcia, "Attributes of Effective Schools for Language Minority Students," *Education and Urban Society* 20 (4), 387–98; E. R. Hollim, J. E. King, and W. C. Hayman, eds. *Teaching Diverse Populations: Formalizing a Knowledge Base* (Albany: SUNY Press, 1994).

3. G. G. Wehlage, et al., *Reducing the Risk: Schools as Communities of Support* (Philadelphia: The Falmer Press, 1989).

4. Terrel Bell, *A Nation at Risk: The Imperative for Educational Reform: An Open Letter to the American People* (National Commission on Excellence in Education, 1983).

Chapter 5

1. P.L. 81–815 provides funds for building school facilities, although the federal government has a long waiting list.

2. This analysis comes from Neil Smelser, *Theory of Collective Behavior* (New York: Free Press, 1961). His theory goes a long way to an understanding of how cultures, in this particular case Indian culture, can change norms, roles, and institutions without changing the basic foundation of Indian culture, values.

3. My students often challenge this statement. I have a simple test. I ask them to name a hero (a person who embodies exemplary characteristics) who lived two hundred years ago (they usually name George Washington), identify his characteristics, and then name a contemporary American hero and identify his characteristics. They are often amazed at how similar in nature these heroes are. They embody societal values.

Chapter 6

1. The school war played out in Madison is not unlike the school wars taking place today in many urban areas where shifting ethnic populations impact neighborhood schools governed and administrated by a former, usually white, majority. Desegretation and busing have not immeasurably changed the ethnic composition of inner-city schools in Boston, Los Angeles, Chicago, or New York, nor does the governance, administration, and faculty reflect the ethnic diversity within these school systems.

Chapter 7

1. Robert Rosenthal, *Pygmalion in the Classroom* (New York: Holt, Rinehart & Winston, 1968).

2. Individual education plans (IEP) are objectives for each student in each subject. Teachers learn to put together learning packets for each subject, so that on any given week, individual students can work on the subject packet and complete the week's work in a few days or over the entire week. It is similar to a contract that students have with teachers that a given amount of work will be finished during class time each week. This allows teachers to individualize instruction to satisfy advanced, average, and below-level students.

Chapter 8

1. I test this hypothesis out almost every term in my classes. I ask students to recall the fifth grade and their teacher. They invariably remember the name because of some personality characteristic they perceived as kind or stern. Whatever the reasons for their assessment, my students report an indelible impression of that grade.

2. The most sought after fields in the Indian community are those in the science and health fields. Jobs are filled by non-Indians because there are not enough Indians to fill positions in medicine, environmental-related fields, resource management, geology, and mineral/mining-related fields.

Chapter 9

1. The most prevalent migration pattern of Indians from reservations resembles *step migration,* a global sociology term used to illustrate population shifts from rural roots to urban cities. Often the shift is generational, in "steps." The first generation to leave the reservation because of job or educational opportunities after World War II settled into bordertowns surrounding the reservation. Some left these bordertowns to seek greater opportunities in the next largest city in the state, and from there to the largest city in the state. This process takes a generation for the transition from reservation to city. However, most will return to more rural areas because it is cheaper, means a less hectic lifestyle, and is more congruent with their lifestyle.

2. Reprinted from *A Nation at Risk: the Imperative for Educational Reform.* 1983 National Commission on Excellence in Education, as reprinted in the *Congressional Record,* v. 129, May 5, 1983 S6096–S6108.

3. Ernest L. Boyer High School: An Agenda for Action: A Report on Secondary Education in America (Carnegie Foundation for the Advancement of Teaching. New York: Harper & Row, 1984).

4. Ibid, part 4, 249–319.

5. National Coalition of Advocates for Students, *Barriers to Excellence: Our Children at Risk,* 1–31, 1985.

6. National Coalition of Advocates for Students, *Barriers to Excellence,* 1–31.

7. Ibid.

8. Ernest L. Boyer, High School: A Report on Secondary Education in America (Carnegie Foundation for the Advancement of Teaching. New York: Harper and Row, 1984), pt. 4, 249–319.

9. Ibid.

10. Ibid.

11. A Twentieth Century Fund: Task Force on Federal Elementary and Secondary Education Policy. Making the grade report. New York, the fund. 1983. Comment by Mr. Hortas quoted in the report.

12. National Coalition of Advocates for Students, *Barriers to Excellence: Our Children at Risk,* 1–31.

Chapter 10

1. Richard J. Herrnstein and Charles Murray, *The Bell Curve* (New York: Free Press, 1995).

2. I turned into a television talk show that had Murray as a guest. A caller identified himself as a white Anglo-Saxon and then asked Murray what was in the white genes that led to a five hundred-year history of genocide committed by whites on the Indians of this continent and/or Hitler in Germany. Murray's response was that the gene was not responsible and that it was like comparing white genes with what you had for dessert that day. Murray is not a historian, so perhaps he should be forgiven, but since the Anglo-Saxons went on the Crusades they have done so in the name of racial superiority. Even the educational codes of many states, including

California, assert that the intelligence of other races is not equal to that of whites, and there is subject to "natural law" or the right of the whites to dominate other races. Perhaps he should start with the argument made five centuries ago between Vittoria, Las Casas, and Sepulvada as to whether American Indians were human, and therefore entitled to property rights. To further emphasize the point, in 1880 Judge Dundy ruled in the Federal District Court against the army in the case of *Standing Bear vs. U.S.* The army contended that Standing Bear was not covered under the Writ of Habeas Corpus and had no right to leave the reservation because he was not human, and consequently the Bill of Rights did not apply to Indians. Judge Dundy declared once and for all that the American Indian is a human being.

3. There is a certain grotesque déjà vu in this proposed policy because of its frightening resemblance to the placement of Indian children in off-reservation boarding schools designed to "eradicate the Indian, but make the man."

4. Ronald Takaki's book *From Distant Shores* contains two papers originally presented by him and Nathan Glazer at the Ethnicity and Public Policy Conference at the University of Wisconsin in 1982. These papers are highly recommended readings because they present two diametrically opposed views of racism and ethnicity.

5. Ironically, it was Indian land and Indian agriculture that eventuated into capitalism because both factors contributed toward over production, i.e. more than could be initially consumed by farmers/and or small communities. The over production led to a market place, the development of capital and cities. See also Max Weber's penetrating analysis, *The Protestant Ethic and the Spirit of Capitalism.*

6. Ronald Takaki quotes Alexis de Tocqueville, *Democracy in America* originally published in 1835 (2 vols. (New York: Charles Scribner's Sons, 1958, 373, 374, 352–53, 364); "What awed Tocqueville," was the ability of white society to deprive the Indians of their rights and exterminate them 'with singular felicity, tranquillity, legally, philanthropically.' As he caught a glimpse of a peculiar horror present in an American racial pattern, he remarked in barbed language: "It is impossible to destroy men with more respect for the laws of humanity."

7. Samuel Bowls and Herbert Gintis. *Schooling in Capitalist America* (New York: Basic Books, 1976), 123.

8. Lester Thurow, an economist at MIT and an avid supporter of capitalism has on many occasions spoken and written eloquently about the deterioration of American education. I am paraphrasing him now, but

I have heard him warn the public on an address he gave over CSPAN (1994) that if the growth of the underclass and undereducated continues, not only will it affect our position in the global economy, but it will seriously contribute to a stagnant American society. Poor people cannot earn sufficient income to buy the home that generates growth in the economy, or save, or pay taxes.

9. Nathan Glazer, an eminent scholar from Harvard, has often argued the case that the institution of education is largely responsible for the strength of the American middle-class as it transformed poor immigrants into the middle-class within several generations. My difficulty with his analysis is that I do not see it applied to racial minorities, especially African Americans and American Indians even during the same era of sizable immigration patterns of the late 1800s to the early 1900s.

Chapter 11

1. National Advisory Council on Indian Education, *Annual Report 1988.* U.S. Government Documents.

2. Ibid.

3. An illustration is a story that comes from Sam Cagey, former tribal chairman of the Lummi in Washington State. Two friends, one Indian and one white, went crabbing. Each filled his bucket and placed it under a tree while they went nearby to have lunch. When they came back, they found that one bucket was almost empty of crabs and the other was filled. The Indian claimed the filled bucket, but the white man said it was his. The Indian said he could prove the filled bucket was his: "Watch the crabs in the filled bucket. See how one has almost climbed to the top? Now watch what the other crabs do. See how they are grabbing him back to the bottom? That's Indian crabs. They either all go out or all stay at the bottom." Now look at the other bucket . There are still a few in there, at the bottom. That's white crabs."

4. I bumped into a colleague at an annual National Indian Education Association who recruits for MIT who relayed this information and wanted to know what I knew about the school these students came from. The only thing I knew was that it was a tribal school on the Navajo reservation. This, and information from other colleagues at Stanford and Dartmouth, suggests that tribal schools have made excellence a goal and a reality.

5. Some people refer to this as the "Harvard connection" (of which I am, proudly one), but I have seen this same networking taking place on

my campus as graduates enter professional fields and call upon the Indians they knew in college to provide technical skills in areas needed by tribal organizations they are working for. Indians are learning and using the "old boy network" with a vengeance.

6. Another example of networking, this time through e-mail. Technology is present and raring to go on Indian reservations, and the Indians use computers, modems, and satellites to communicate and learn from one another. The days of rural reservation isolation are coming to a screeching halt.

7. Indian Country owes a lot to the Office of Economic Opportunity. It funded both Rough Rock Demonstration School and the Navajo Community College at a time when neither the Bureau of Indian Affairs nor the U.S. Department of Education gave any serious consideration to funding a tribally controlled education system.

8. Testimony of Lawrence Gishey, president of Navajo Community College, before the Oversight Hearing on Tribally Controlled Community Assistance Act, Committee on Education and Labor, April 21, 1990.

9. Testimony of Paul Boyer, Carnegie Foundation Special Report on Tribal Colleges, before the Oversight Hearing on Tribally Controlled Community Assistance Act, Committee on Education and Labor, April 21, 1990.

10. Ibid., 44.

11. Ibid., 45.

12. Ibid., 45.

Epilogue

1. Even more galling, California passed legislation in 1860 that in effect sanctioned Indian slavery while ironically voting with northern states opposing slavery in the South.

2. This figure is approximate, pending petitions for tribal recognition. Due to the Tillie Hardwick successful Supreme Court decisions, twenty-eight terminated tribes in California filed for reinstatement to federally recognized tribes. Seventeen were re-instated because Tillie Hardwick argued that the conditions for accepting termination were not met by the federal or state government.

Some tribes were literally wiped out by the gold rush. The census in 1900 counted 15,000 California Indians. In 1850, the approximate California Indian population was estimated by Sherbroke Cook as 275,000 to

300,000. A reasonable estimate is that 90 percent of the indigenous people of California were killed during the gold rush era of 1849–1859. Contrary to popular myth, most were killed by bullets, not by smallpox. California even paid a bounty for dead Indians.

Because of the fragmentation brought about by these early Californians, many tribes have never been federally recognized. In the last decade, legislation was passed to permit petitions for federal recognition. Twenty tribes have completed that process, but only one has succeeded attaining federal recognition in California, the Timbisha Shoshone.

3. This is not a minor point. For centuries, the federal and state governments have treated Supreme Court decisions affirming tribal sovereignty and concomitant federal to tribal government relationship as inconvenient or at the very least, given it lip-service. The tribes insist the federal government keep its word and not allow the various states and the Bureau of Indian Affairs to direct Indian policy.

4. The resolution stated that states be directed through an executive order (from the president) to "collect, aggregate, analyze and disseminate to local, state and national level data on Indian student achievement, graduation, dropout, retention, student transfer and enrollment date by race, gender, and grade level." Currently, there is an apparent lack of consistent and comprehensive data on Indian education achievement and to assure Indian students have equitable educational outcomes by assuring accountability of public funds used by local education agencies for the education of Indian students."

5. Usually federal appropriations for state programs have 1 percent set aside for Indian Country, and within that 1 percent are funds to enable tribes to develop or educate their own personnel. For instance, Indian Health has education funds to train health professionals, as do Economic Development, Commerce, etc.

6. There is a valid concern that funds allocated to different agencies do not have the same impact that funds collected in a centralized funding agency would have. However, experience has shown that funding can be drastically reduced when it is centralized, and often when a tribe seeks programmatic money from one agency and is turned down, it has alternative funding sources. For instance, suppose the Department of Education turns down a proposal for a technical program in a tribal school. The Department of Commerce, Agriculture, or Housing might see a benefit to funding a technical program in the tribal school.

7. The White House Conference on Indian Education hereby requests "That Congress fund the Tribally Controlled College Act at the full authorized amount of $5,280 per student." Some tribal colleges receive half of the stipulated amount in the Tribally Controlled Community College Act.

INDEX